More of ...

The Best of

BITS &
PIECES

COMPILED AND EDITED BY
ROB GILBERT, PH.D.

THE ECONOMICS PRESS, INC.
12 DANIEL ROAD
FAIRFIELD, NEW JERSEY 07004-2565

More of The Best of Bits & Pieces
Library of Congress Catalog Card Number: 97-60808

More of The Best of Bits & Pieces
ISBN 0-910187-11-8

The Economics Press, Inc.
Fairfield, New Jersey

More of *The Best of* **BITS & PIECES** is dedicated to the four former editors whose skill, commitment, and hard work have brought hope, motivation, inspiration, and humor to millions of **BITS & PIECES** readers over the past 30 years:

MARV GREGORY

JOHN L. BECKLEY

ROBERT KLEINMANNS

ARTHUR F. LENEHAN

The Magical Book

Once upon a time, there was a man who received a magical book. The very first time he opened the book he saw written on the first page:

"THE BOOK OF AHA'S AND HA HA'S"

He wasn't quite sure what that meant, but he was intrigued, so he opened the book and started reading it. Then something very exciting happened—lightbulbs went on in his mind, bells rang in his head, and a smile emerged on his face.

The book worked its magic no matter when it was opened and no matter what page it was opened to.

The man began to realize that every time he read this book, he always came away with insights, ideas, and a light-hearted feeling.

He cherished his book. Often when he had trouble and couldn't put his thoughts into words, or he couldn't make sense of his feelings or couldn't figure out what to do, he would take the book in his hands, close his eyes, and open the book. Then he would open his eyes and the first passage his eyes fell upon seemed to be just what he needed to read.

The man went on reading his book for many weeks and one day he discovered that it possessed another magical quality. No matter how often he read the book, he always found passages he had never seen before.

He gained a great deal from this book.

The book motivated him when he needed motivation, consoled him when he needed consolation, and inspired him when he needed inspiration.

The man kept the book on his desk in a special place. He was convinced that the wisdom he gained from the book had helped him become healthy, wealthy, and wise.

And as you may have guessed . . .

The man lived happily ever after.

What you might not have guessed is . . .

THIS IS THAT MAGICAL BOOK
and
IT'S NOW IN YOUR HANDS.

Rob Gilbert, Ph.D.
Editor

Why More of . . .?

Because you can't get too much of a good thing!

A few short years ago, in his preface to the first-ever compilation drawn from nearly 25 years of *BITS & PIECES—the magazine that motivates the world* and 10 years of its companion publication *LEADERSHIP*, editor Arthur F. Lenehan wrote these prophetic words:

While we present it as "the best" of our efforts, we're well aware that some of our readers may have other ideas. If you have a favorite essay, story, proverb, or bit of humor that you feel belongs here, drop us a line and let us know. It might lead to **More of *The Best of* BITS & PIECES**.

Might?! While Art isn't known as a master of understatement, here he wins the gold medal.

It seems as if every reader (including the 200-plus employee-owners of The Economics Press) had a "favorite" that did not appear in the original volume. From around the company and around the country and around the world, they wrote. They phoned. They faxed. And when we opened our Internet Web site—**http://www.epinc.com**—and gave folks a cyberspace place to share their favorite quotables, the responses really poured in.

And with those responses came the requests for The Economics Press to put together another book of, well, more.

So here you have it. MORE inspiration. MORE insights. MORE success secrets.

Continuing in the tradition of *The Best of* **BITS & PIECES**, this copy of **More of** . . . puts at your fingertips an ALL-NEW collection of thoughts, anecdotes, stories, proverbs, one-liners, and gentle humor to inspire, motivate, delight, and celebrate success.

As is always the goal, **More of** *The Best of* **BITS & PIECES** highlights and celebrates all the positive qualities of humanity: The will to win . . . to transcend the usual . . . to search for excellence . . . to achieve . . . to grow . . . to seek truth and beauty . . . to live by the Golden Rule.

This new compilation has more pages and many more entries than its predecessor. That's due, in many respects, to readers like you. And so, once again, an invitation:

If you have a favorite essay, story, proverb, or bit of humor that you would like to share, drop us a line and let us know.

Write to us at The Economics Press, 12 Daniel Road, Fairfield, NJ, 07004-2565 USA. Fax: 973-227-3558. E-mail: edit@epinc.com

And while you're at it, give us your thoughts about the title of the next compilation. Or perhaps **Even More of** *The Best of* **BITS & PIECES** is just the right touch.

Alan D. Yohalem
President

CONTENTS

SUBJECT	PAGE	SUBJECT	PAGE

❖ ❖ ❖ ABILITY

NICCOLÒ PAGANINI (1782-1840), one of the greatest violinists of all time, was about to perform before a sold-out opera house. He walked out on stage to a huge ovation and felt that something was terribly wrong.

Suddenly he realized that he had someone else's violin in his hands. Horrified, but knowing that he had no other choice, he began.

That day he gave the performance of his life.

After the concert, Paganini reflected to a fellow musician, "Today, I learned the most important lesson of my career. Before today, I thought *the music was in the violin*; today I learned that *the music is in me.*"

PEOPLE OF GREAT ABILITY do not emerge, as a rule, from the happiest background. So far as my own observation goes, I would conclude that ability, although hereditary, is improved by an early measure of adversity and improved again by a later measure of success.

C. NORTHCOTE PARKINSON (1909-1993)
British historian and writer

ACHIEVEMENT ❖ ❖ ❖

I long to accomplish a great and noble task, but it is my chief duty to accomplish small tasks as if they were great and noble.

HELEN KELLER (1880-1968)
Educator and writer

———————

…ake a wrong, but they did make a pretty
g…

———————

The mother of American statesman Bernard Baruch used to motivate him by telling him, "No one is better than you, but you are no better than anyone else until you do something to prove it."

———————

WE CAN'T ANTICIPATE SUCCESS in the things that we do. You may write a sentence that will become chiseled in marble on someone's library, but you don't know that when you write it. And that's usually not the best motivation behind that kind of creative activity anyway. I think if it's fantastic and fun and adventurous, that gives us our best time, and very often will give us our best results also.

JOHN WILLIAMS
Composer

———————

Doing things by halves is worthless because it may be the other half that counts.

———————

Most of us can do more than we think we can, but we usually do less than we think we do.

———————

2

ACHIEVEMENT FORMULA

C + B = A
Conceive + Believe = Achieve
What you CONCEIVE in your mind
and BELIEVE in your heart
you will ACHIEVE in reality.

There are two ways to reach the top of an oak tree—you climb it or sit on an acorn and wait.

People will know you're serious when you produce.

MUHAMMAD ALI
Former heavyweight boxing champion

Bite off more than you can chew,
*   then chew it.*
Plan more than you can do,
*   then do it.*
Point your arrow at a star,
*   take your aim, and there you are.*

Arrange more time than you can spare,
*   then spare it.*
Take on more than you can bear,
*   then bear it.*
Plan your castle in the air,
*   then build a ship to take you there.*

ACTION ❖ ❖ ❖

Do it.

Do it right.

Do it right now.

God gives every bird its food, but He does not throw it in the nest.

A MATH PROBLEM

QUESTION: Three frogs sat on a log and one decided to jump off. How many frogs were left on the log?

Answer: Three.

Explanation: Although almost everyone answers "two," the correct answer is "three." Just because that frog *decided* to jump off the log does not necessarily mean that it actually *did* it.

Is there a gap between what you *decide* to do and what you *actually* do?

An ounce of practice is worth a pound of theory.

It is not so much what we know as how well we use what we know.

Backbone beats wishbone every time.

THERE ARE FOUR general things you can do with your hands: 1) put them in your pockets for safekeeping; 2) fold them in apathy; 3) wring them in despair; or 4) lay them on a job that needs doing.

The person who won't read has no advantage over the person who can't.

THE WORD "begin" is full of energy. The best way to get something done is to begin. It's truly amazing what tasks we can accomplish if only we begin. You're never finished if you forever keep beginning.

REV. CLIFFORD WARREN
Welsh clergyman

I am only one,
But still I am one.
I cannot do everything,
But I can do something,
And because I cannot do everything
I will not refuse to do
The something that I can do.

EDWARD E. HALE (1822-1909)
Clergyman and writer

The best time to plant a tree was 20 years ago. The second best time is now.

CHINESE PROVERB

5

WHAT COUNTS in management is action. One executive puts it this way: "To look is one thing. To see what you look at is another. To understand what you see is a third. To learn from what you understand is still something else. But to act on what you learn is all that really matters."

Helen Chapman, president, General Federation of Women's Clubs: "Let us help mold the world, and not be molded by it!"

---

*I spent a fortune
On a trampoline,
A stationary bike
And a rowing machine.
Complete with gadgets
To read my pulse,
And gadgets to prove
My progress results,
And others to show
The miles I've charted—
But they left off the gadget
To get me started!*

You can't build a reputation on what you're going to do.

HENRY FORD (1863-1947)
Founder, Ford Motor Co.

PEOPLE say to me, "You were a roaring success. How did you do it?" I go back to what my parents taught me. Apply yourself. Get all the education you can, but then, by God, do something. Don't just stand there, make something happen.

LEE IACOCCA
Auto executive

❖ ❖ ❖ **ADVERTISING**

THE OWNER of a hair salon in a small town enjoyed the serenity of knowing that his was the only salon in town. He was responsible for cutting and styling the hair of just about every resident. His livelihood enabled him to live comfortably.

Unfortunately, progress invaded the town, and right across the street from the busy little hair salon sprang one of those new full-service salon franchises.

Immediately, the media campaign began: Ads in newspapers, magazines, and billboards announced, "EVERYTHING FOR $6.00! $6.00 haircuts, $6.00 perms, $6.00 manicures, everything for $6.00." Soon all his customers—his neighbors—began visiting the salon across the street, and the man's business sat empty.

Desperate, he hired a consultant. "I'm finished," he cried. "It's impossible for me, little me, to compete with them."

The consultant squinted his eyes at the salon across the street. "Not just yet, not just yet." With that he picked up the phone and dialed the town's only billboard company. "Yes, on top of our salon . . . big letters . . . the message? WE FIX $6.00 HAIR-CUTS."

———————

Advertising is what makes you think you longed all your life for something you've never heard of before.

———————

7

ADVICE ◆ ◆ ◆

Many people who give admirable advice are incapable of taking it.

NOVELIST SINCLAIR LEWIS was supposed to deliver an hour-long lecture to a group of college students who planned to be writers. Lewis opened his talk with a question:

"How many of you really intend to be writers?"

All hands went up.

"In that case," said Lewis, "my advice to you is to go home and write."

With that, he left.

A word to the wise is sufficient. A word to the unwise is resented.

AGE ◆ ◆ ◆

We do not stop playing because we grow old; we grow old because we stop playing.

Age is something that doesn't matter unless you are a cheese.

BILLIE BURKE (1884-1970)
Actress

Think young. Aging is for wine.

What's a wrinkle but merely a line,
That happens to appear after some time.
Should we laugh or should we cry,
Or should we stop and wonder why;
Or might we simply accept life's lease—
The more we live, the more we crease.

ANNA APOIAN
Educator

The most aggravating thing about the younger generation is that I no longer belong to it.

ALBERT EINSTEIN (1879-1955)
Physicist

Age is a quality of mind.
If you have left your dreams behind,
If hope is cold,
If you no longer look ahead,
If your innermost fires are dead—
Then you are old.

But if from life you take the best,
And if in life you keep the jest,
If love you hold,
No matter how the years go by,
No matter how the birthdays fly—
You are not old.

ON THE OCCASION of her 100th birthday in 1993, a woman was being interviewed by a reporter. She answered all the questions put to her until the reporter asked her to what she attributed the fact that she'd reached such a milestone.

There was a rather long pause, and then she replied, "I guess the main reason I got to be 100 years old is that I was born in 1893."

———

COMEDIAN GEORGE BURNS once said: "Tennis is a game for young people. Until age 25, you can play singles. From there until age 35, you should play doubles. I won't tell you my age, but when I played, there were 28 people on the court—just on my side of the net."

———

The advantage age has over youth is that youth knows nothing about being old, whereas old knows all about being young.

———

I look forward to being older, when what you look like becomes less and less the issue, and what you are is the point.

SUSAN SARANDON
Actress

———

Immaturity can last a lifetime.

ROBERT HALF
Personnel recruiting executive

———

❖ ❖ ❖ ANGER

Anyone can be angry—that is easy. But to be angry with the right person, to the right degree, at the right time, for the right purpose, and in the right way—that is not easy.

ARISTOTLE

The Nichomachean Ethics

Your temper is one of your most valuable possessions. Don't lose it.

MANY YEARS AGO a senior executive of the then Standard Oil Company made a wrong decision that cost the company more than $2 million. John D. Rockefeller was then running the company. On the day the news leaked out, most of the executives of the company were finding various ingenious ways of avoiding Rockefeller, lest his wrath descend on their heads.

There was one exception, however; he was Edward T. Bedford, a partner in the company. Bedford was scheduled to see Rockefeller that day, and he kept the appointment, even though he was prepared to listen to a long harangue against the man who made the error in judgment.

When Bedford entered the office, the powerful head of the gigantic Standard Oil empire was bent over his desk busily writing with a pencil on a pad of paper. Bedford stood silently, not wishing to interrupt. After a few minutes Rockefeller looked up.

"Oh, it's you, Bedford," he said calmly. "I suppose you've heard about our loss?"

Bedford said that he had.

"I've been thinking it over," Rockefeller said, "and before I

11

ask the man to discuss the matter, I've been making some notes."

Bedford later told the story this way:

"Across the top of the page was written, 'Points in favor of Mr. _____.' There followed a long list of the man's virtues, including a brief description of how he had helped the company make the right decision on three separate occasions that had earned many times the cost of his recent error.

"I never forgot that lesson. In later years, whenever I was tempted to rip into anyone, I forced myself first to sit down and thoughtfully compile as long a list of good points as I possibly could. Invariably, by the time I finished my inventory, I would see the matter in its true perspective and keep my temper under control. There is no telling how many times this habit has prevented me from committing one of the costliest mistakes any executive can make—*losing his temper.*

"I commend it to anyone who must deal with people."

STRANGE BUT TRUE . . .

Your temper is something you never get rid of by losing.

THE CHINESE tell a story based on three or four thousand years of wisdom. Two merchants were arguing heatedly in the midst of a crowd. A stranger, noting the depth of their anger, expressed surprise that no blows were being struck. His friend explained, "The man who strikes first admits that his ideas have given out."

❖ ❖ ❖ APPRECIATION

Nobody notices what I do, until I don't do it.

ARNOLD BENNETT, the British novelist, had a publisher who boasted about the extraordinary efficiency of his secretary. One day while visiting the publisher's office, Bennett asked the secretary: "Your boss claims you're extremely efficient. What's your secret?"

"It's not my secret," said the secretary. "It's his." Each time she did something for him, no matter how insignificant, she explained, he never failed to acknowledge and appreciate it. Because of this, she took infinite pains with her work.

Creativity is so delicate a flower that praise tends to make it bloom, while discouragement often nips it in the bud. Any of us will put out more and better ideas if our efforts are appreciated.

ALEX F. OSBORN
Advertising executive

❖ ❖ ❖ ASSUMPTIONS

IN 1884, a young man from America died while on a visit to Europe. His grieving parents returned with the body.

They were heartbroken. They had loved their son very much. After the funeral, they began to discuss some kind of memorial to his memory—not a tombstone or ornate grave, but a living memorial, something that would help other young men like their son.

After considering many alternatives, they decided that something in the field of education would be most appropriate. It

13

would be the kind of memorial that would go on year after year, helping educate young people. That would be the best kind of tribute to their son's memory.

They arranged an appointment with Charles Eliot, then president of Harvard University. He received the quite ordinary-looking couple in his offices, asking what he could do for them.

They told him about the death of their son. They explained that they wanted to establish a memorial to his memory—something that would help others to get an education.

Eliot looked at the unpretentious couple with some impatience. "Perhaps you have in mind a scholarship," he said.

"No," said the woman, her mild manner belying the quickness and sharpness of her mind. "We were thinking of something more substantial than that—perhaps a new building or so . . . ."

"I must explain to you," said Eliot with what seemed a patronizing air, "that what you suggest costs a great deal of money. Buildings are very expensive." Obviously, Eliot did not think that from their appearance they were capable of that kind of donation.

There was a pause, then the lady rose slowly and said, "Mr. Eliot, what has this entire university cost?"

Eliot shrugged and muttering, stated a figure that amounted to several million dollars.

"Oh, we can do better than that," said the lady, who now had seemed to make up her mind about the entire thing. "Come, dear," she motioned to her husband, "I have an idea." And they left.

The following year President Eliot of Harvard learned that the plain, unpretentious couple had contributed $26 million for a memorial to their son. The memorial was to be named Leland Stanford Jr. University.

———————

AFTER AN ACCIDENT, a woman stepped forward and prepared to help the victim. She was asked to step aside by a man who announced,

"Step back please! I've had a course in first aid."

The woman watched his procedures for a few moments, then tapped him on the shoulder. "When you get to the part about calling a doctor," she said, "I'm already here."

♦ ♦ ♦ **ATTITUDE**

Alter your attitude and you can alter your life.

If you go by other people's opinions or predictions, you'll just end up talking yourself out of something. If you're running down the track of life thinking that it's impossible to break life's records, those thoughts have a funny way of sinking into your feet.

CARL LEWIS
Olympic track champion

The world is a mirror that reflects our own face. Frown at it and it will show you a sourpuss. Laugh at it and it will be your jolly friend.

A SICKLY WIDOW had two sons on whom she relied for financial support.

One son sold umbrellas. The first thing the mother did every morning was to look out to see if the sun was shining or if it looked like it was going to rain. If it was cloudy, her spirits were good because there was a chance that it might rain and her son would sell some umbrellas. But if the sun was shining, she was miserable all day because no umbrellas would be sold.

15

The widow's other son sold fans. Every morning that it looked like rain, she would get depressed because without the sun's heat, no one was likely to buy fans.

No matter what the weather was, the widow had something to fret about.

While commiserating with a friend one day, the friend remarked, "Perk up. You've got it made. If the sun is shining, people will buy fans; if it rains, they'll buy umbrellas. All you have to do is change your attitude. You can't lose."

When that simple thought sank in, the widow lived happily ever after.

FATHER BRIAN CAVANAUGH
Adapted from *Sower of Seeds*
Paulist Press

BELIEF ❖ ❖ ❖

MOST SUCCESSFUL PEOPLE are people who take risks—calculated risks—but nevertheless, risks.

Consider the case of the rising young executive who suddenly found himself unemployed when his company went through a downsizing.

When he asked "Why me?" the vice president, who was the young man's superior, explained that he was too conservative in the way he did his job. "Things have gotten more competitive," the VP explained. "Our people have to look at things from different angles and they have to take risks. And when they take risks, they have to believe they'll succeed. That's where you come up short."

For six months the young man tried to get a job and failed. Then one day he met a retired circus tightrope walker. The two had something in common—time on their hands. Before long, the unemployed executive became an accomplished tightrope walker.

He became so good that he and his circus mentor were asked to participate in a televised charity event at Niagara Falls, and the young man invited his former boss to attend. "I'll show him who can take risks," he said.

All went well at the event. The young man successfully crossed the falls on the tightrope, followed by his circus mentor, who also pushed a wheelbarrow across. The vice president congratulated the young man and then dared him to cross over the falls again, this time pushing the wheelbarrow. "You can do it if you believe you can," said the vice president.

"Do you believe I can?" the young man asked his former boss.

"Yes, I do," the vice president replied.

"Okay," said the young man, "get in the wheelbarrow."

———————————

Believe in something larger than yourself.

BARBARA BUSH
Former First Lady of the U.S.

———————————

The first person who has to believe in you is you.

———————————

In all this world, there is nothing more upsetting than the clobbering of a cherished belief.

CHARLES M. SCHULZ
Cartoonist

———————————

17

BREAKTHROUGHS ❖ ❖ ❖

AT A SPECIAL OLYMPICS TRACK MEET, a young girl had just won the 50-yard dash and was jumping up and down, all excited.

She yelled out to her parents, "Look, Mom and Dad, I won."

Her parents instantly burst into tears.

At the awards ceremony the young girl proudly stood there as a medal was placed around her neck.

Then she ran over to her parents, who were now crying even more than before.

The three of them hugged, as her parents kept crying.

A meet official who had watched this whole scene became concerned and went over to the parents and said, "Excuse me. Is there anything wrong?"

Through her tears, the mother said, "No, nothing's wrong. Everything's right. We just heard our daughter speak for the very first time."

The Wright brothers flew right through the smoke screen of impossibility.

CHARLES F. KETTERING (1876-1958)
Inventor

SOMETIMES YOUR BIGGEST weakness can become your biggest strength. Take, for example, the story of one 10-year-old boy who decided to study judo despite the fact that he had lost his left arm in a devastating car accident.

The boy began lessons with an old Japanese judo master. The boy was doing well, so he couldn't understand why, after three months of training, the master had taught him only one move.

"Sensei," the boy finally said, "shouldn't I be learning more moves?"

"This is the only move you know, but this is the only move you'll ever need to know," the sensei replied.

Not quite understanding, but trusting in his teacher, the boy kept training.

Several months later, the sensei took the boy to his first tournament. Surprising himself, the boy easily won his first two matches. The third match proved to be more difficult, but after some time, his opponent became impatient and charged; the boy deftly used his one move to win the match. Still amazed by his success, the boy was now in the finals.

This time his opponent was bigger, stronger, and more experienced. For a while, the boy appeared to be overmatched. Concerned that the boy might get hurt, the referee called a time-out. He was about to stop the match when the sensei intervened.

"No," the sensei insisted, "let him continue."

Soon after the match resumed, his opponent made a critical mistake: He dropped his guard. Instantly, the boy used his move to pin him. The boy had won the match and the tournament. He was a champion.

On the way home, the boy and the sensei reviewed every move in each match. Then the boy summoned the courage to ask what was really on his mind.

"Sensei, how did I win the tournament with only one move?"

"You won for two reasons," the sensei answered. "First, you've almost mastered one of the most difficult throws in all of judo. And second, the only known defense for that move is for your opponent to grab your left arm."

The boy's biggest weakness had become his biggest strength.

———————

DO YOU REMEMBER the four-minute mile? They'd been trying to do it since the days of the ancient Greeks. Someone found the old records of how the Greeks tried to accomplish this. They had wild animals chase the runners, hoping that would make them run faster. They tried tiger's milk: not the stuff you get down at the supermarket, I'm talking about the real thing.

Nothing worked, so they decided it was physically impossible for a human being to run a mile in four minutes. Our bone structure was all wrong, the wind resistance was too great, our lung power was inadequate. There were a million reasons.

Then one day one human being proved that the doctors, the trainers, and the athletes themselves were all wrong. And, miracle of miracles, the year after Roger Bannister broke the four-minute mile, 37 other runners broke the four-minute mile. And the year after that, 300 runners broke the four-minute mile!

HARVEY MACKAY
Entrepreneur and writer
in *Speechwriter's Newsletter*

BREVITY ❖ ❖ ❖

Unless you are brief, your complete plan of thought will seldom be grasped. Before you reach the conclusion, the reader or listener has forgotten the beginning and the middle.

HORACE (65-8 B.C.)
Latin poet and satirist

"Brevity is not only the soul of wit," said Samuel Butler, "but the soul of making oneself agreeable, and of getting on with people, and indeed of everything that makes life worth living."

THE LEGENDARY Supreme Court Justice Oliver Wendell Holmes, Jr., wrote his opinions standing beside a special high desk. "Mr. Justice, why do you write your opinions standing up?" a new assistant asked him one day.

"It's very simple," said the famed jurist. "If I sit down, I write a long opinion and don't come to the point as quickly as I could. If I stand up, I write as long as my knees hold out. When my knees give out, I know it's time to stop."

❖ ❖ ❖ **BUSINESS**

A FATHER brought his son, just out of school with an MBA, into the family business as a 25 percent owner. "I think you'll learn the business sooner if you start in the factory," said the father.

"Dad, the factory is automated, we get reports, and I don't need to spend any time there," said the son.

"Okay, perhaps you should start in sales. That's a good way to find out what the customers want."

"Dad, I have an MBA! We don't knock on any doors. Come on, let's be professional businessmen here."

"Okay," said the father, "tell me what you want."

"Buy me out," replied the son.

The Jokesmith

THE WORLD'S SHORTEST BUSINESS POEM
Hired.
Tired.
Fired.

21

More important than getting ahead of your rivals is getting along with them.

FINDING A BRIGHT SPOT in the ominous task known variously these days as "rightsizing" or "workplace reengineering" isn't easy. But one consultant brought in to help remaining managers through the process of reducing the workforce while maintaining productivity added a contemporary twist to the old classic.

"What does the optimist say about the glass and the water?" he asked.

"It's half full," was the reply.

"And what does the pessimist say?" he queried.

"It's half empty."

"And what does the process reengineer have to say about it?"

Silence—until the consultant revealed the new additional answer: "Looks like you've got twice as much glass as you need there."

CAREERS ❖ ❖ ❖

Headline on an advertisement recruiting managers: *"What you need is a good swift kick in the career."*

When I told my father I was going to be an actor, he said, "Fine, but study welding just in case."

ROBIN WILLIAMS
Actor and comedian

AT THE HEIGHT OF HIS CAREER, the late Henry Fonda was asked what he considered the most important thing a young actor could learn.

"How to become an old actor," Fonda replied.

❖ ❖ ❖ **CHALLENGES**

WHEN YOU WALK into the office of T.J. Rodgers, founder and CEO of Cypress Semiconductor, you'll see a sign:

"Be realistic—demand the impossible."

The greatest leaders are pioneers—visionaries with the courage to demand the impossible from themselves and others in order to realize their bold visions. They challenge people to look beyond perceived limitations and imagine things as they could be—to take the impossible and not only make it possible, but also make it a practical reality.

Henry Ford, one of the greatest technological innovators of the 20th century, was just such a person. In the book *Developing The Leader Within You* (Thomas Nelson Publishers), author John C. Maxwell tells the following story to illustrate how Ford could demand the impossible—and get it:

"Automobile genius Henry Ford once came up with a revolutionary plan for a new kind of engine. We know it today as the V-8. Ford was eager to get his great new idea into production. He had some men draw up plans and presented them to the engineers.

"As the engineers studied the drawings, one by one they came to the same conclusion. Their visionary boss just didn't know much about the fundamental principles of engineering. He'd have to be told gently—his dream was impossible.

"Ford said, 'Produce it anyway.'

23

"They replied, 'But it's impossible.'

" 'Go ahead,' Ford commanded, 'and stay on the job until you succeed, no matter how much time is required.'

"For six months they struggled with drawing after drawing, design after design. Nothing. Another six months. Nothing. At the end of the year Ford checked with his engineers, and once again they told him that what he wanted was impossible.

"Ford told them to keep going. They did. And they discovered how to build a V-8 engine."

For me, it's the challenge—the challenge to try to beat myself, to do better than I did in the past. I try to keep in mind not what I have accomplished but what I have to try to accomplish in the future.

JACKIE JOYNER-KERSEE
Olympic track champion

Challenges make you discover things about yourself that you never really knew. They're what make the instrument stretch— what make you go beyond the norm.

CICELY TYSON
Actress

The key to life is accepting challenges. Once someone stops doing this, he's dead.

BETTE DAVIS (1908-1989)
Actress

24

"MEN WANTED for hazardous journey. Low wages, long hours . . . ." This advertisement was placed in the early 1900s by E. Shackleton—he was looking for adventurers to help him discover the South Pole. The ad drew 5,000 brave candidates. The lesson learned: People respond when they're challenged to greatness.

As journalist H. L. Mencken once wrote, "It is the feeling of exerting effort that exhilarates us, as a grasshopper is exhilarated by jumping. A hard job, full of impediments, is thus more satisfying than an easy job."

❖ ❖ ❖ **CHANGE**

Change is inevitable, except from a vending machine.

HOW DO YOU go on an effective diet? How do you stop smoking? How do you stop drinking?

In short, you do it and it's done. Then you work . . . for the rest of your life to stay on the weight-maintenance, nonsmoking, or booze-free wagon.

A while back, I came across a line attributed to IBM founder Thomas Watson. If you want to achieve excellence, he said, you can get there today. As of this second, quit doing less-than-excellent work.

The idea is profound.

Suppose you're a waiter and, for your own future's sake (not because of pressure from the clowns who run the restaurant), you decide to set a matchless standard for service. How? You do it. Now.

Sure, you'll be clumsy at first. You'll get a lot of it wrong.

You'll need to read up, listen to audiotapes, take classes, tune in to online electronic chat rooms, visit other restaurants to collect clues. And you'll need to keep doing such things to maintain your edge (as an opera singer or professional athlete does) until the day you hang up your corkscrew.

Nonetheless, you can become excellent in a nanosecond, starting with your first guest tonight. Simply picture yourself, even if it's a very fuzzy picture, as the greatest waiter ever—and start acting accordingly. Put yourself in lights on Broadway, as a galaxy-class waiter; then perform your script with derring-do.

Does it sound wild? Silly? Naive? Maybe, but it isn't. The first 99.9 percent of getting from here to there is the determination to do it and not to compromise, no matter what sort of roadblocks those around you (including peers) erect.

The last 99.9 percent (I know it adds up to more than 100 percent—that's life) is working like the devil to (1) keep your spirits up through the inevitable storms, (2) learn something new every day, and (3) practice that something, awkward or not and no matter what, until it's become part of your nature.

What holds for the waiter also holds for the manager of the six-person department or the chief executive of the 16,000-person firm.

How long does it take you, as boss, to achieve world-class quality? Less than a nanosecond to attain it, a lifetime of passionate pursuit to maintain it.

Once the fire is lit, assume you've arrived—and never, ever look back or do anything, no matter how trivial, that's inconsistent with your newfound quality persona.

TOM PETERS
The Pursuit of Wow!
Random House

———————

People's minds are changed through observation and not through argument.

WILL ROGERS (1879-1935)
Humorist

When you're through changing, you're through.

BRUCE BARTON (1886-1967)
Advertising executive

♦ ♦ ♦ CHARACTER

Character is much easier kept than recovered.

People rarely disclose their character so clearly as when they describe someone else's.

People and cars are very much alike. Some are right at home racing up the hills; others run smoothly only going downhill. And when you hear one knocking all the time, it's a sure sign something is wrong under the hood.

A good way to judge people is by observing how they treat those who can do them absolutely no good.

HOW DELIGHTFUL IS THE COMPANY of generous people, who overlook trifles and keep their minds instinctively fixed on whatever is good and positive in the world about them. People of smaller caliber are always carping. They are bent on showing their own superiority, their knowledge or prowess or good breeding. But magnanimous people have no vanity, they have no jealousy, they have no reserves, and they feed on the true and the solid wherever they find it. And what is more, they find it everywhere.

VAN WYCK BROOKS (1886-1963)
Essayist and critic

A garden filled with virtues,
Now wouldn't that be nice;
If we could cultivate the good
And weed out all the vice!

P.S. and S.R. MAMCHAK
2002 Gems of Educational Wit & Humor
Parker Publishing

To have courage without pugnacity,
To have conviction without bigotry,
To have charity without condescension,
To have faith without credulity,
To have love of humanity without
*   mere sentimentality,*
To have meekness with power,
*   and emotion with sanity,*
That is brotherhood.

CHARLES EVANS HUGHES (1862-1948)
Chief Justice of the United States

❖ ❖ ❖ **COMMUNICATION**

Half the world is composed of people who have something to say and can't, and the other half have nothing to say and keep on saying it.

ROBERT FROST (1874-1963)
Poet

Discussion is an exchange of knowledge; argument an exchange of ignorance.

ROBERT QUILLEN

HUMPHREY BOGART and Lauren Bacall were in a nightclub when Harry Cohn, president of Columbia Pictures, came over to their table and whispered a few words to Bogart.

Bogart turned to her and beamed, "The picture's a hit."

"What makes you so sure?" she asked.

"Because Harry referred to it as 'our picture,'" Bogart explained. "If it was a flop, he'd have said 'your picture.'"

DR. HERBERT H. CLARK, a psychologist from The Johns Hopkins University, discovered that it takes the average person about 48 percent longer to understand a sentence using a negative than it does to understand a positive or affirmative sentence.

This is confirmation of something every successful person knows: The secret of good communication is positive affirmation. It is not what you can't or won't do that interests people, but what you *can* or *will* do.

29

Say what you mean, mean what you say, but don't say it mean.

A lot of people don't have much to say, and that's fine. The trouble with some of them is you have to listen a long time to find it out.

When you have spoken the word, it reigns over you. When it is unspoken, you reign over it.

WHEN REMBRANDT'S famous painting, *The Night Watch*, was restored and returned to Amsterdam's Rijksmuseum, the curators performed a simple, yet remarkable experiment. They asked visitors to submit questions about the painting. The curators then prepared answers to over 50 questions, ranking the questions according to popularity.

Some of these questions focused on issues which curators usually don't like to include: How much does the painting cost? Has this painting ever been forged? Are there mistakes in the painting? Other questions focused on traditional artistic issues: Why did Rembrandt paint the subject? Who were the people in the painting? What techniques did Rembrandt pioneer in this particular work?

In a room next to the gallery which held the painting, the curators papered the walls with these questions (and answers). Visitors had to pass through this room before entering the gallery.

The curious outcome was that the average length of time people spent viewing the painting increased from six minutes to over half an hour. Visitors alternated between reading questions and answers and examining the painting. They said that the questions encouraged them to look longer, to look closer, and to remember more. The questions helped them create richer ideas about the painting and to see the painting in new ways. Like a series of magnets, the questions attracted the visitors' thoughts to fresh ideas.

How can questions produce such dramatic results? Essentially, the questions put visitors into a ready-to-learn frame of mind by stimulating curiosity.

The word "question" originates from the Latin root, *quaestio,* which means "to seek." Inside the word *"question"* is the word "quest," suggesting that within every question is an adventure, a pursuit which can lead us to hidden treasure.

TOM WUJEC
Five Star Mind
Doubleday

The three most important words for a successful relationship are communication, communication, and communication.

The value of the average conversation could be enormously improved by the constant use of four simple words: "I do not know."

ANDRÉ MAUROIS (1885-1967)
French writer

Speak softly and sweetly. When your words are soft and sweet, they won't be as hard to swallow if you have to eat them.

A good conversationalist is not one who remembers what was said, but says what someone wants to remember.

JOHN MASON BROWN
Theater critic

We communicate with our bodies, especially the hands. How many people, when asked to describe a corkscrew, can do it without twirling their finger?

A gossip is one who talks to you about others; a bore is one who talks to you about himself; and a brilliant conversationalist is one who talks to you about yourself.

LISA KIRK
Singer

A VISITOR to Great Britain got into a taxi and looked appealingly at the driver. "I'm not good at English," he began, "and I've lost the word."

"You mean you've forgotten the name of the street where you want to go?" asked the driver.

The man nodded, tapping his head as though to shake the missing word loose. Finally he smiled and said, "Take me to the wife of King Street."

The taxi driver lost no time in driving him to Queen Street.

Some people leave without saying good-bye. Others say good-bye and take forever to leave.

TWO OLD MEN are sitting on a park bench in the Danish countryside, when a car stops, and the driver politely asks, in German, for assistance. The men shrug and shake their heads. The driver asks again, this time in French. No answer. He asks a third time in English. Still no answer. Frustrated, the man drives away.

After a while, one old-timer says to the other, "I wish I could speak a second language."

"What for?" asks his friend. "That guy spoke three languages, and it didn't help him."

The Jokesmith

Profanity is the effort of a feeble mind to express itself forcefully.

MOTHER MOUSE was crossing a path in the woods with her three little babies. She noticed a big cat crouching behind a bush.

The cat eyeballed Mother Mouse. Mother Mouse eyeballed the cat. Then Mother Mouse bellowed out, "Woof, woof, woof." The cat got so scared that it jumped up and ran away.

Mother Mouse proudly turned to her babies and said, "Now do you see the value of learning a second language?"

❖ ❖ ❖ COMPASSION

ONE AFTERNOON YEARS AGO, reporters and officials gathered at a Chicago railroad station to await the arrival of the Nobel Prize winner.

He stepped off the train—a giant of a man, six-feet-four, with bushy hair and a large mustache.

As cameras flashed, the officials came up with hands outstretched and began telling him how honored they were to meet him. He thanked them and then, looking over their heads, asked if he might be excused for a moment. He walked through the crowd with quick steps until he reached an elderly woman who was having trouble trying to carry two large suitcases.

He picked up the bags in his big hands and smiling, escorted the woman to a bus. As he helped her aboard, he wished her a safe journey. Meanwhile, the crowd tagged along behind him. He turned to them and said, "Sorry to have kept you waiting." The man was Dr. Albert Schweitzer, the famous missionary-doctor who had spent his life helping the poorest of the poor in Africa.

Said a member of the reception committee to one of the reporters: "That's the first time I ever saw a sermon walking."

Everybody wants to right the world; nobody wants to help his neighbor.

HENRY MILLER (1891-1980)
Writer

If we could read the secret history of our enemies, we should find in each man's life sorrow and suffering enough to disarm all hostility.

HENRY WADSWORTH LONGFELLOW (1807-1882)
Poet

THERE'S A CHINESE PROVERB that says, "You cannot prevent the birds of sorrow from flying over your head, but you can prevent them from building nests in your hair."

Dr. Karl Menninger, the famous psychiatrist, would agree with that. After giving a lecture on mental health, Menninger took questions from the audience.

"What would you advise a person to do," asked one man, "if that person felt a nervous breakdown coming on?"

Most people expected him to reply, "Consult a psychiatrist." To their surprise, he replied, "Lock up your house, go across the railway tracks, find someone in need, and do something to help that person."

A story by Alexander Woollcott shows what can happen when such advice is followed:

A nurse found herself one day attempting to console a grief-stricken mother who had just lost her only child. The woman was sitting in stunned silence, gazing blindly into space as tears streamed down her cheeks.

"Mrs. Norris," the nurse asked her, "have you noticed the little boy sitting in the hall next to your daughter's room?"

Mrs. Norris had not.

"There," said the nurse, "is a case." She pointed out that the little boy's mother had been brought to the hospital in an ambulance about a week earlier from a shabby, one-room apartment where she and the boy had lived since their arrival in the U.S. from Europe three months before.

The nurse had learned that the mother and son had no family. They had lost all their people in the old country and knew no one in America. They only had each other.

Every day, the nurse explained, the little boy kept a vigil at his mother's side, hoping that she would come out of her coma. "She never will," the nurse said to Mrs. Norris. "Death has taken her along with your daughter."

"Now it is my duty," said the nurse, "to go out and tell that little fellow that, at the age of seven, he is all alone in the world." She paused, then turned plaintively to Mrs. Norris. "I don't suppose," she said hesitantly, "that you could go out and tell him for me?"

Mrs. Norris stood up, dried her tears, walked out into the hall, and put her arms around the boy. She had found someone in need and did something about it.

The next day she took the homeless boy to her childless

home. In the darkest moment of their lives, a grief-stricken mother and a little boy became beacons of love and hope for each other.

We are not primarily put on this earth to see through one another, but to see one another through.

PETER DE VRIES
Writer

COMPETITION ❖ ❖ ❖

Everything now being done is going to be done differently; it's going to be done better, and if you don't do it, your competitor will.

SYNDICATED COLUMNIST Sydney J. Harris used a sports analogy to point out that just a little more concentration can yield significantly greater results. "Consider two major league baseball players," he said. "One hits .275 for the season. The other hits .300. The one hitting .300 may easily have a contract awarding him twice as much as the one hitting .275. Yet the difference between the two, over the season, is only one extra hit in 40 times at bat."

The comparisons are endless: A racehorse that wins by a nose, a marathon runner who wins by a step, a field-goal kicker who carries his team to victory on the strength of a single point, or the basketball player who hits the winning shot at the buzzer.

Harris used the analogy to illustrate the point that in any field where there are a lot of skilled, highly trained competitors, nobody is twice as good as everyone else. You don't have to be;

a 5- or 10-percent advantage will put you far ahead of the pack.

The Executive Speechwriter Newsletter

❖ ❖ ❖ **COMPLIMENTS**

The best way to knock a chip off someone's shoulder is to pat the person on the back.

———

THE CHINESE HAVE A PROVERB that says, "A bit of fragrance clings to the hand that gives flowers."

This also goes for verbal or written bouquets. Say something nice to someone, and a bit of niceness will cling to you.

They say you can't get something for nothing. You can't give something for nothing, either. People who find good things to say about others will find others saying good things about them.

———

THE DUKE OF WELLINGTON, the British military leader who defeated Napoleon at Waterloo, was not an easy man to serve under. He was brilliant, demanding, and not one to shower his subordinates with compliments.

Yet even Wellington realized that his methods left something to be desired. In his old age a young woman asked him what, if anything, he would do differently if he had his life to live over again.

Wellington thought for a moment, then replied, "I'd give more praise."

———

COMPUTERS ❖ ❖ ❖

Some people spend so much time logged on to their computer that they're more at risk of getting a computer virus than a real one.

"JUST GIVE US a few days," the repair technician said. "When we have the part, our computer will call your home to let you know."

"I'm not home during the day," the customer said. "But I do have an answering machine."

"Sorry, sir," the technician said. "Our computer won't talk to a machine."

The Random House Book of Jokes and Anecdotes
Random House

I GUESS I SEE the Internet as sort of like the wilderness of the Wild West. Eventually civilization will move in and make rules about what is or is not acceptable. And as systems and services grow, the place will become more civilized in its own interest. But like the West, there will always remain some interesting wilderness areas to visit.

VINT CERF
Senior Vice President, MCI

AND IT CAME TO PASS that the people of the earth banded together to design and build the ultimate computer.

Every technology, discipline, and philosophy was represented. Money was no object. The capacity was reported in "ZIPS"— zillions of instructions per second. They programmed it with every known fact.

Meanwhile, a second team was charged with fashioning the ultimate questions—questions to both test the machine and to learn the nature of our existence.

Years later, both teams made their reports. The second team, after many agonizing discussions, agreed on the ultimate question that the computer should be asked. It was simply *Why?* The question was entered into the computer.

The machine blinked and whirred and went into a processing cycle that was too rapid to measure. On and on it went for days, weeks, months, and finally, the great truth, the answer appeared on the screen.

It read: "Because."

The Jokesmith

C:\DOS
C:\DOS\RUN
RUN\DOS\RUN

You can't fail to get along with a computer; it will never turn on you, it will never insist on talking about what it wants to talk about or doing what it wants to do. It will never find you boring, never forget to call, never ask a favor.

GREG EASTERBROOK

CONFIDENCE ♦ ♦ ♦

SOMEHOW I can't believe there are many heights that can't be scaled by a man who knows the secret of making dreams come true. This special secret, it seems to me, can be summarized in four Cs.

They are Curiosity, Confidence, Courage, and Constancy, and the greatest of these is CONFIDENCE. When you believe a thing, believe it all over, implicitly and unquestioning.

WALT DISNEY (1901-1966)
Film and theme park entrepreneur

———————

Class is an aura of confidence that is being sure without being cocky. Class has nothing to do with money. Class never runs scared. It is self-discipline and self-knowledge. It's the surefootedness that comes with having proved you can meet life.

ANN LANDERS
Syndicated columnist

———————

BISHOP FULTON SHEEN once went shopping at a department store. He got on an elevator at the fifth floor and pushed the button for the sixth. Before the doors closed, a woman rushed on and as the elevator rose she said, "I didn't want to go up. I wanted to go down."

She turned to Bishop Sheen and added, "I didn't think I could go wrong following you."

"Madam," replied Bishop Sheen, "I only take people up, not down."

———————

◆ ◆ ◆ **COURAGE**

When people share their fears with you, share your courage with them.

It doesn't take much to buy a ticket and go in and watch the bullfight. But it takes a whole lot to jump into the ring and fight the bull.

YOU GAIN STRENGTH, courage, and confidence by every experience in which you really stop to look fear in the face. You are able to say to yourself, "I lived through this horror. I can take the next thing that comes along." You must do the thing you think you cannot do.

ELEANOR ROOSEVELT (1884-1962)
First Lady of the U.S.

Those who lose riches lose much, but those who lose courage lose all.

THERE ARE PEOPLE who put their dreams in a little box and say, "Yes, I've got dreams, of course, I've got dreams." Then they put the box away and bring it out once in a while to look in it, and yep, they're still there.

These are great dreams, but they never even get out of the box. It takes an uncommon amount of guts to put your dreams on the line, to hold them up and say, "How good or how bad am I?" That's where courage comes in.

ERMA BOMBECK (1927-1996)
Syndicated columnist

There are too many people praying for mountains of difficulty to be removed, when what they really need is courage to climb them.

I CAN SAY, "I am terribly frightened, and fear is terrible and awful, and it makes me uncomfortable, so I won't do that because it's uncomfortable."

Or I could say, "Get used to being uncomfortable. It is uncomfortable doing something that's risky."

But so what? Do you want to stagnate and just be comfortable?

BARBRA STREISAND
Entertainer

COURTESY ❖ ❖ ❖

Courtesy is the shortest distance between two people.

"BE KNOWN FOR your courtesy—it alone can make you worthy of praise," said Baltasar Gracián, the worldly Spanish Jesuit priest who lived from 1601 until 1658.

"Courtesy is the best part of culture," he wrote, "a kind of enchantment that wins the goodwill of all, just as rudeness wins only scorn and universal annoyance. . . .

"Better too much courtesy than too little, or the same sort for everyone, for that would lead to injustice. Treat your enemies with courtesy, and you'll see how valuable it really is. It costs little, but pays a nice dividend—those who honor are honored. Politeness and a sense of honor have this advantage: We bestow them on others without losing a thing."

KNOWLEDGE, ability, experience are of little avail in reaching high success if courtesy be lacking. Courtesy is the one passport that will be accepted without question in every land, in every office, in every home, in every heart in the world. For nothing commends itself so well as kindness; and courtesy is kindness.

GEORGE D. POWERS

❖ ❖ ❖ CREATIVITY

AFTER PERIODS DURING which one has actively tried to solve a problem, but has not succeeded, the sudden right orientation of the situation, and with it the resolution, tend to occur at moments of extreme mental passivity . . . .

A well-known physicist in Scotland once told me that this kind of thing is generally recognized by physicists in Britain. "We often talk about the Three B's," he said, "the Bus, the Bath, and the Bed. That's where the great discoveries are made in our science."

WOLFGANG KÖHLER
The Task of Gestalt Psychology
Princeton University Press

Discovery consists of looking at the same thing as everyone else and thinking something different.

ALBERT SZENT-GYÖRGYI (1893-1986)
Biochemist

LIFE ENERGY FLOWS when we create, or when we help another person's creativity flower by encouraging them in some way.

Think of the sense of joy and satisfaction that one can derive from the simple act of planting flowers, cooking a meal, writing a poem, solving a problem, painting a picture, dressing with flair, or doing your job to the best of your abilities.

Creativity brings us life, and by using our creativity we help bring the world into being.

JOAN BORYSENKO
Psychologist and writer

Be brave enough to live creatively. The creative is the place where no one else has ever been. You have to leave the city of your comfort and go into the wilderness of your intuition. You can't get there by bus, only by hard work, risking, and by not quite knowing what you're doing. What you'll discover will be wonderful: *yourself*.

ALAN ALDA
Actor

A LOT OF US tend to get into a comfortable rut and stay there. Getting out can pay dividends for ourselves and our employers.

One way to do this is to travel to new places and see new things. Business consultant Rosabeth Moss Kanter recommends to her clients that they permit managers to attend seminars in fields different from their own. She believes this is how true innovation can be spawned.

The success of Clarence Birdseye is a case in point. It wasn't until he took a vacation to a bitter-cold part of North America that he came up with the idea of freezing vegetables. The idea came to him while watching how the Eskimos would quickly freeze their food (naturally) for consumption later. The idea created the now famous and hugely successful brand of products that bears his name.

You can break out of your comfortable rut by walking around your plant or office, asking questions, and seeing what other people do. Remember, if you get accustomed to thinking a certain way, or seeing things a certain way, you'll stay unless something jolts you out of it.

———————

WHEN NAPOLEON HILL finished his book, it had the working title: *The Thirteen Steps to Riches*. The publisher, however, wanted a better selling title; he wanted a million-dollar name for the book. He kept calling Hill every day for the new title, but even though he had tried about 600 different possibilities, none of them was good enough.

Then one day the publisher phoned and said, "I've got to have the title by tomorrow. If you don't have one, I have. It's *Use Your Noodle and Get the Boodle!*"

"That's awful," shouted Hill. "That title is ridiculous."

"Well, that's it, unless you get a better one by tomorrow morning," was the reply.

That night Hill had a talk with his subconscious mind. In a loud voice, he said, "You and I have gone a long way together. You've done a lot of things for me—and some things to me. But I've got to have a million-dollar title, and I've got to have it tonight. Do you understand that?"

For several hours, he thought but was unproductive. Frustrated, he went to bed. About two o'clock, he woke up as though someone had shaken him. As he came out of his sleep, a phrase glowed in his mind. He jumped to his typewriter and typed the phrase. Then he grabbed the phone and called the publisher. "We've got it," he shouted, "a million-dollar title."

And he was right. For *Think and Grow Rich* has sold millions of copies since that day and has become a classic in the self-help field.

———————

CRITICISM ❖ ❖ ❖

How much easier it is to be critical than to be correct.

BENJAMIN DISRAELI (1804-1881)
British Prime Minister

It's easier to criticize than to create. That's why there are more critics than creators.

HOW A PERSON REACTS to criticism often means the difference between success and failure. Take the case of Ole Bull, the famous Norwegian violinist of the past century.

His practical father, a chemist, sent him to the University of Christiania to study for the ministry and forbade him to play his beloved violin. He promptly flunked out and, defying his father, devoted all his time and energy to the violin. Unfortunately, though he had great ability, his teachers were relatively unskilled, so by the time he was ready to start his concert tour, he wasn't prepared.

In Italy, a Milan newspaper critic wrote: "He is an untrained musician. If he be a diamond, he is certainly in the rough and unpolished."

There were two ways Ole Bull could have reacted to that criticism. He could have let it make him angry, or he could learn from it. Fortunately he chose the latter. He went to the newspaper office and asked to see the critic. The astounded editor introduced him. Ole spent the evening with the 70-year-old critic, asked about his faults, and sought the older man's advice on how to correct them.

Then he canceled the rest of his tour, returned home, and spent the next six months studying under really able teachers. He practiced hours upon hours to overcome his faults. Finally, he returned to his concerts and, when only 26, became the sensation of Europe.

A long-winded novelist once asked author Ambrose Bierce to critique his latest book. Bierce had one comment: "I think the covers are too far apart."

If it is painful for you to criticize someone, you're safe in doing it; if you take pleasure in it, hold your tongue.

We judge ourselves by what we think we are capable of doing; others judge us by what we do.

❖ ❖ ❖ CURIOSITY

EDISON WAS ASKED to sign a guest book that had the usual columns for name and address, as well as one for "Interested in."

In this last column Edison entered the word: "Everything."

CLIFTON FADIMAN (General Editor)
The Little, Brown Book of Anecdotes
Little, Brown & Company

I have no particular talent; I am merely extremely inquisitive.

ALBERT EINSTEIN (1879-1955)
Physicist

THE LINES WAITING to get into P.T. Barnum's circus were unusually long. One time, the story goes, in order to move those inside through faster, Barnum hung a sign over one of the exits that read, "This way to the egress." Many people in the crowd, eager to see what kind of strange animal an egress was, passed through the door and found themselves on the street.

"HOW COME your arm is in a sling? Is it broken?" one traveler asked another.

"Yes, unfortunately, it is."

"An accident?"

"No, I broke it when I was trying to pat myself on the back."

"No kidding! Why would you be giving yourself a pat on the back?"

"For minding my own business."

CUSTOMER SERVICE ✦ ✦ ✦

The way employees treat customers reflects the manner in which they're being treated by management.

JAMES A. PERKINS
Senior Vice President, Federal Express

Motivate them, train them, care about them, and make winners out of them . . . . If we treat our employees correctly, they'll treat the customers right. And if the customers are treated right, they come back.

J.W. MARRIOTT, JR.
Chairman, Marriott Corporation

FROM A SIGN posted in L.L. Bean's original store in Freeport, Maine:

A Customer is the most important person ever in this office
. . . in person or by mail.

A Customer is not dependent on us . . . we are dependent on him.

A Customer is not an interruption of our work . . . he is the purpose of it. We are not doing a favor by serving him . . . he is doing us a favor by giving us the opportunity to do so.

A Customer is not someone to argue or match wits with. Nobody ever won an argument with a Customer.

A Customer is a person who brings us his wants.
It is our job to handle them profitably for him and ourselves.

Some Japanese and American executives were discussing the state of the world economy and one American asked what the Japanese regarded as the most important language for world trade. The American assumed that the answer would be English, but one member of the Japanese contingent smiled and replied, "My customer's language."

The mark of an exceptional company is how it treats exceptions.

JOE DEGEORGE
Regional Sales Director, Federal Express

DETAILS ❖ ❖ ❖

JOKO-SENSEI, a teacher at the Zen Center of San Diego, tells that one morning she was working putting finishing touches on a remodeled kitchen at the Zen Center of Los Angeles, when the teacher Maezumi-roshi walked in to see how things were going.

"Everything's going fine," she said, "There are only a few details to finish up."

At this point the roshi scratched his head. "Only a few details?" he asked, looking puzzled. "But details are all there are."

RICK FIELDS
Chop Wood, Carry Water
Jeremy T. Tarcher

DETERMINATION ❖ ❖ ❖

Some people succeed because they are *destined* to succeed, but most people succeed because they are *determined* to succeed.

The difference between the impossible and the possible lies in a person's determination.

TOMMY LASORDA
Baseball manager

When life knocks you down, try to fall on your back because if you can look up, you can get up.

LES BROWN
Motivational speaker

❖ ❖ ❖ **DIETING**

Brain cells come and brain cells go, but fat cells live forever.

Worried about gaining weight over the holidays? Remember: It's not how much weight you gain between Thanksgiving and New Year's. What really matters is how much weight you gain between New Year's and Thanksgiving.

The second day of the diet is always easier than the first. By the second day you're off it.

JACKIE GLEASON (1916-1987)
Comedian and actor

There's a new diet that is all the rage. You can eat all you want of everything you don't like.

The five-word weight-loss formula:

Eat less and exercise more.

Just about the time your income gets to the point where food prices don't matter—calories do.

DISCIPLINE ❖ ❖ ❖

I believe everybody is creative, and everybody is talented. I just don't think that everybody is disciplined. I think that's a rare commodity.

AL HIRSCHFIELD
Caricaturist

Some people regard discipline as a chore. For me, it is a kind of order that sets me free to fly.

JULIE ANDREWS
British actress

Perhaps the most valuable result of all education is the ability to make yourself do the thing you have to do when it ought to be done, whether you like it or not. It is the first lesson that ought to be learned and is probably the last lesson a person learns thoroughly.

THOMAS HUXLEY (1825-1895)
British biologist

NO HORSE GETS anywhere till he is harnessed.

No steam or gas ever drives anything until it is confined.

No Niagara is ever turned into light and power until it is tunneled.

No life ever grows great until it is focused, dedicated, disciplined.

HARRY EMERSON FOSDICK (1878-1969)
Religious leader

❖ ❖ ❖ DREAMS

Hold fast to dreams, for if dreams die, life is a broken-winged bird that cannot fly.

LANGSTON HUGHES (1902-1967)
Poet and writer

Don't be afraid of the space between your dreams and reality. If you can dream it, you can make it so.

BELVA DAVIS
Newscaster

Those who dream by day are cognizant of many things that escape those who dream only by night.

EDGAR ALLEN POE (1809-1849)
Writer and poet

❖ ❖ ❖ EDUCATION

Education is the ability to listen to almost anything without losing your temper or your self-confidence.

ROBERT FROST (1874-1963)
Poet

I'm attending school only until it becomes available on CD-ROM.

ANONYMOUS STUDENT

The three Rs—reading, 'riting, and 'rithmetic—are no longer enough. We must add the three Cs—computing, critical thinking, and the capacity for change.

FRED GLUCK
Former managing director, McKinsey and Co.

———————

What skills will be required for tomorrow? Nobody knows. The important thing is to keep acquiring new ones. We're in an environment where education—for life, for everyone—is the game.

TOM PETERS
Business writer and speaker

———————

A TEACHER asked a highly intelligent but rebellious student: "Bob, what's the difference between ignorance and indifference?"

He shrugged and said, "I don't know and I don't care."

TOM MORRIS
True Success
Grosset-Putnam

———————

THE MOST IMPORTANT LESSON I learned in college was during the first moments of the first class on the first day . . . .

With my notebook open to the very first page, I waited for my English professor to begin.

Without a word, she turned to the board and wrote:

"College is a fountain of knowledge where some come to drink, more come to sip, but, unfortunately, most come just to gargle."

ROB GILBERT
Editor, *Bits & Pieces*

———————

TV talk-show host Johnny Carson once asked baseball great Yogi Berra how he liked school. Berra replied, "Closed."

I hear and I forget, I see and I remember, I do and I understand.

CHINESE PROVERB

Someone once asked Benjamin Franklin what condition of humankind deserved the most pity. His reply: "A lonesome person on a rainy day who does not know how to read."

In the end we will conserve only what we love. We will love only what we understand. We will understand only what we are taught.

SENAGALESE PROVERB

A TEACHER WAS TRYING to impress upon the first grade pupils that good penmanship was important.

"Remember," the teacher said, "if you don't learn to sign your name, you'll have to pay cash for everything when you grow up."

❖ ❖ ❖ **EFFORT**

If you have tried to do something and failed, you are vastly better off than if you tried to do nothing and succeeded.

Ever wonder why somebody doesn't try softer?

LILY TOMLIN
Comedian

Remember this your lifetime through,
Tomorrow there will be more to do.

And failure waits for those who stay
With some success made yesterday.

Tomorrow you must try once more
And even harder than before.

Be like a duck—keep calm and unruffled on the surface, but paddle like the devil underneath.

EGOTISM ✦ ✦ ✦

Egotists are people who think too much of themselves and too little of others.

A COMPOSER was invited to a dinner party at the home of a Hollywood executive.

"I'd rather not go," he told a friend. "I know exactly what will happen. As soon as the dinner is over, he'll ask me to play the piano. I'll have to spend the rest of the night entertaining his guests."

The friend, however, persuaded the composer to attend anyway. After dinner he waited defiantly for his host to ask him to play. The latter extended no such invitation. After an hour or so the composer's defiance melted. When another hour passed and the host still had not asked him to play, the composer grew increasingly annoyed. Finally, as the evening was drawing to a close, he became downright angry.

"What does he mean, not asking me to play?" he said to his friend. "Is he trying to humiliate me in front of all these people?"

❖ ❖ ❖ EMPATHY

To handle yourself, use your head; to handle others, use your heart.

An executive with a lot of personal appeal usually has the gift of empathy. Webster defines it as the capacity to participate in another's feelings or ideas. You put yourself in someone else's shoes. You listen with an understanding heart and mind. If you have empathy, you cannot only understand others, you can inspire them.

A FRIGHTENED LITTLE GIRL, hospitalized for a tonsillectomy, clung tightly to a battered, one-eyed teddy bear as the doctor approached her bedside to announce that it was time for the operation. A nurse moved to take the bear, but the doctor said, "Leave Teddy there. He needs some attention too."

Hours later, when the child regained consciousness, Teddy was snuggled against the pillow—and across his missing eye was the neatest bandage a skillful surgeon could devise.

ONE DAY an eight-year-old boy went to the pet store with his dad to buy a puppy. The store manager showed them to a pen where five little furry balls huddled together.

After a while, the boy noticed one of the litter all by itself in an adjacent pen.

The boy asked, "Why is that puppy all alone?"

The manager explained, "That puppy was born with a bad leg and would be crippled for life, so we're going to have to put him to sleep."

"You're going to kill this little puppy?" the boy said sadly while patting it.

"You have to realize that this puppy would never be able to run and play with a boy like you."

After a short conversation with his boy, the dad told the manager that they wanted to buy the puppy with the bad leg.

"For the same amount of money, you could have one of the 'healthy' ones. Why do you want this one?"

To answer the manager's question, the boy bent over and pulled up the pants on his right leg, exposed the brace beneath, and said, "Mister, I want this one because I understand what he's going through."

———————————

HER LITTLE GIRL was late arriving home from school so the mother began to scold her daughter, but stopped and asked, "Why are you so late?"

"I had to help another girl. She was in trouble," replied the daughter.

"What did you do to help her?"

"Oh, I sat down and helped her cry."

CAROL WARNER
The Last Word
Prentice Hall

———————————

❖ ❖ ❖ ENCOURAGEMENT

BEFORE FAMED POET Langston Hughes received national recognition, he worked at the fashionable Wardman Park Hotel in Washington, D.C., busing tables at the restaurant. The pay wasn't much, but it provided his meals and he didn't care about the rest.

What did matter was that one day he learned one of the leading poets, Vachel Lindsay, was staying at the hotel. He had read Lindsay's poems and admired him. Lindsay was both a minstrel and a missionary, a people's poet like Carl Sandburg.

Hughes worked up the courage to drop three of his poems at Lindsay's dinner plate, unable to say more than that he liked Lindsay's poems and that these were his own poems. Then he fled toward the kitchen.

Lindsay gave a reading that night in the hotel theater. Hughes couldn't go to the reading because the management wouldn't allow black people to attend. When Hughes showed up for work the next morning, reporters were waiting for him. They told him Lindsay had read his poems aloud and praised them to the large audience.

The press interviewed Hughes and took his picture. Although he had had some poems published, he was relatively unknown. His name soon spread to the whole country.

At the hotel desk, Hughes found that Lindsay, too shy himself to try to see Hughes, had left for him a beautiful set of Amy Lowell's biography of poet John Keats. On the first blank page, Lindsay had written a long letter filled with encouragement.

Hughes never forgot Lindsay's kindness and encouragement. It helped him overcome many obstacles in his career.

Reach down and lift others up. It's the best exercise you can get.

HOW MUCH IS ENCOURAGEMENT worth? Joseph Priestley failed as a preacher and turned to teaching. On a vacation he happened to meet Benjamin Franklin, who was twice his age. Franklin saw possibilities for other than grade-school teaching in him. "You have just the abilities to write a history of electricity," Franklin told him, "and I will help you start by lending you my books and notes."

Flattered, Priestley rushed to the task. In a year he had finished the first history of electricity. He became a man of science, discovered oxygen, and developed the first carbon dioxide fire extinguisher, all thanks to a few words of praise and encouragement from Ben Franklin.

A helping word to one in trouble is often like a switch on a railroad track—but one inch between a wreck and smooth rolling prosperity.

H.W. BEECHER (1813-1887)
Clergyman

DESIRING TO EXPLAIN the principles of happiness and success, the Rev. Norman Vincent Peale decided to write a book. Writing a brief introduction was easy; organizing a thousand fragmentary ideas into a unified theme was something else.

One day a friend of Peale's found him with his head in his hands and the manuscript scattered all over a big table. "It's no use," the minister said. "I may be a preacher, but I'm no writer. Never again."

"Who's going to publish it?" asked his friend.

"I don't know," said Peale. "Nobody, probably. No publisher in his right mind would touch it."

At one point he grew so disgusted that he threw the whole manuscript into the wastebasket. Peale's wife Ruth rescued the manuscript. She gave it to her father-in-law to read, and he passed it along to a friend who worked in a publishing house. The friend carried it to his office, and there it stayed. Weeks went by. No reaction came from the publisher.

"You see," said Peale to his wife, "I told you it was no good."

"It's a good book, Norman," she kept saying. "Sooner or later, somebody is going to realize it."

She was right. Her dejected husband wrote to ask for the return of the manuscript. But by this time the publishers had made up their minds. Contracts and suggestions for revisions were placed before the astonished Peale. Before he knew quite what had happened, the book was on the press.

The book was titled *A Guide to Confident Living*. In the next four years it went through 25 printings. Rev. Peale went on to write dozens of other books that have sold millions of copies.

---

*The greatest good you can do for others is not just to show your riches but to reveal to them **their** own.*

BENJAMIN DISRAELI (1804-1881)
British prime minister

❖ ❖ ❖ **ENTHUSIASM**

Manufacture enthusiasm as you go and grow.

MAGGIE KUHN (1905-1995)
Founder, The Gray Panthers

Enthusiasm is one of the most powerful engines of success. When you do a thing, do it with your might. Put your whole soul into it. Stamp it with your own personality. Be active, be energetic, be enthusiastic and faithful, and you will accomplish your object. Nothing great was ever achieved without enthusiasm.

RALPH WALDO EMERSON (1803-1882)
Philosopher, essayist, and poet

EXAMPLE ❖ ❖ ❖

FOR MANY YEARS, Monterey, a California coast town, was a pelican's paradise. As the fishermen cleaned their fish, they flung the offal to the pelicans. The birds grew fat, lazy, and contented. Eventually, however, the offal was utilized, and there were no longer snacks for the pelicans.

When the change came, the pelicans made no effort to fish for themselves. They waited around and grew gaunt and thin. Many starved to death. They had forgotten how to fish for themselves.

The problem was solved by importing new pelicans from the south, birds accustomed to foraging for themselves. They were placed among their starving cousins, and the newcomers immediately started catching fish. Before long, the hungry pelicans followed suit, and the famine was ended.

AS A BOY in the Middle West, I used to amuse myself by holding a stick across a gateway that the sheep had to pass through.

After the first few sheep had jumped over the stick, I took it away; but all the other sheep leaped through the gateway over an imaginary barrier. The only reason for their jumping was that those in front had jumped.

The sheep is not the only animal with that tendency. Almost all of us are prone to do what others are doing, to believe what others are believing, to accept without question, the testimony of prominent people.

DALE CARNEGIE
Public Speaking (Association Press)

TALKING THE TALK
VS
WALKING THE WALK

I'd rather see a sermon
Than hear one any day.

I'd rather once you walk with me
Than merely show the way.

The eye's a better pupil
And more willing than the ear.

Fine counsel is confusing
But the example's always clear.

I soon can learn to do it
If you let me see it done.

I can see your hands in action
But your tongue too fast may run.

And the lectures you deliver
May be very fine and true.

But I'd rather get my lesson
By observing what you do.

For a person must understand you
And the high advice you give.

But there's no misunderstanding
How you act and how you live.

EDGAR A. GUEST (1881-1959)
Writer

EXCELLENCE ❖ ❖ ❖

EXCELLENCE IS AN ACT won by training and habituation. We do not act rightly because we have virtue or excellence, but rather we have those because we have acted rightly.

We are what we repeatedly do.

Excellence, then, is not an act, but a habit.

ARISTOTLE (384-322 B.C.)
Greek philosopher

If you refuse to accept anything but the best, you get it more often.

My philosophy is that not only are you responsible for your life, but doing the best at this moment puts you in the best place for the next moment.

OPRAH WINFREY
vision personality

EXPRESSION ❖ ❖ ❖

Of all the things you wear, your expression is the most important.

A smile goes a long way, but you have to start it on its journey.

Smile—it adds to your face value.

64

❖ ❖ ❖ FAILURE

CHARLES F. KETTERING, the inventor, once pointed out that you can learn how to fail intelligently.

"Once you've failed," said Mr. Kettering, "analyze the problem and find out why, because each failure is one more step leading up to the cathedral of success. *The only time you don't want to fail is the last time you try.*"

Failure is success if we learn from it.

MALCOLM FORBES (1919-1990)
Publisher

There is no failure except in no longer trying.

GEORGE BERNARD SHAW tried writing novels before writing plays. They weren't successful and one rejected manuscript was tossed into a corner of his humble living quarters in London, where rodents nibbled at it in the night. Later Shaw commented: "Even the mice couldn't finish it."

Failure is the opportunity to begin again more intelligently.

Defeat isn't bitter, if you don't swallow it.

ONE OF THE KEY characteristics of successful people is how they view failure. Successful people rarely see failure as fatal; they see

65

it as feedback. When they don't get the desired result, they learn from the experience and try, try, again.

The most successful authors, inventors, actors, etc., have developed the ability to deal with massive amounts of rejection. High achievers rarely think of failure as an end in itself. Instead, they believe in delayed success. A loser says, "I can't do it," while a winner says, "I can't do it yet."

ROB GILBERT
Editor, *Bits & Pieces*

FAITH ♦ ♦ ♦

Fear knocked at the door.

Faith answered.

No one was there.

———

THE MINISTER was talking about the relationship between fact and faith.

"That you are sitting before me in this church," he said, "is fact. That I am standing here, speaking from this pulpit, is fact. That I believe anyone is listening to me is faith."

———

A NASA AGENCY OFFICIAL at Kennedy Space Center was explaining to a reporter how a module carrying human beings would land on Mars. The reporter asked how the module would return to earth.

"That involves a highly complex plan," the space agency representative said. "It begins with the words, 'Our Father, who art in Heaven.' "

———

Getting ahead in a difficult profession requires avid faith in yourself. You must be able to sustain yourself against staggering blows. There is no code of conduct to help beginners. That is why some people with mediocre talent, but with great inner drive, go much further than people with vastly superior talent.

SOPHIA LOREN
Italian actress

———————

FEW PEOPLE RECOGNIZE the name Walter Hunt. Yet industrial historians consider Hunt one of the few authentic geniuses the United States has produced.

Walter Hunt was an inventor and was responsible for more practical and successful inventions than any other American. Among the many inventions that flowed from his fertile mind were the fountain pen, rifle, sewing machine, paper collar, and burglar and fire alarms.

Yet Hunt, born in 1796, died in poverty, practically unknown.

His paper collar, first designed when cotton became scarce during the American Civil War, was laughed at. But by the beginning of the 20th century, nearly 40 years after his death, over 400 million were being worn each year in the U.S. alone.

Hunt's lockstitch sewing machine, designed in 1834, was never promoted by Hunt because he feared it would put thousands of seamstresses out of work. He did not have the imagination to see that eventually it would create more jobs than it displaced. Years later, when sewing machines were being sold commercially, Hunt was told it was too late for him to claim the rights to his invention.

Likewise, another inventor is credited with designing the breech-loading, cartridge-firing rifle. Though Hunt invented the rifle, it carries the name of the man who marketed it, Winchester.

Walter Hunt's brilliant mind could have made him rich and

famous. Instead, he died broke and disillusioned. Why? Some say that for all his genius Hunt had a tragic flaw, a weakness that haunted him all his life. *He was said to have lacked the courage of his convictions—lacked faith in himself and his ideas.*

FAMILY ❖ ❖ ❖

There is no doubt that it is around the family and the home that all the greatest virtues, the most dominating virtues of human society, are created, strengthened, and maintained.

WINSTON CHURCHILL (1874-1965)
British prime minister

ERNIE BANKS, the Chicago Cubs Hall of Fame baseball player, always remembered the way his father worked and sacrificed to give him the chance to play baseball. Every day his father left the house before dawn and got home after dark. He worked so many hours that he hardly ever saw sunlight. When Ernie signed his first contract with the Cubs, he sent a three-word telegram to his dad: "We did it!"

At age four children know all the questions, and at age 14 they know all the answers.

SYNDICATED COLUMNIST Erma Bombeck once wrote a piece that likened children to kites.

"You spend a lifetime trying to get them off the ground. You run with them until you're both breathless. They crash. They hit the rooftop. You patch and comfort, adjust, and teach. You watch them lifted by the wind and assure them that someday they'll fly.

"Finally, they are airborne. They need more string and you keep letting it out. But with each twist of the ball of twine, there is a sadness that goes with joy. The kite becomes more distant, and you know it won't be long before that beautiful creature will snap the lifeline that binds you two together and will soar as it is meant to soar, free and alone. Only then do you know that you did your job."

One of the oldest human needs is having someone wonder where you are when you don't come home at night.

MARGARET MEAD (1901-1978)
Anthropologist

THE POET COLERIDGE was visited by an admirer one day. During the conversation the subject got around to children.

"I believe," said the visitor, "that children should be given a free rein to think and act and thus learn at an early age to make their own decisions. This is the only way they can grow into their full potential."

"Come see my flower garden," said Coleridge, leading the man outside. The visitor took one look and exclaimed, "Why, that's nothing but a yard full of weeds!"

"It used to be filled with roses," said Coleridge, "but this year I thought I'd let the garden grow as it willed without tending to it. This is the result."

MARTIN BUXBAUM
Writer

You know your children are growing up when they stop asking

69

you where they came from and refuse to tell you where they're going.

One hundred years from now
It will not matter
What kind of car I drove,
What kind of house I lived in,
How much money I had in my bank account,
Nor what my clothes looked like.

But one hundred years from now
The world may be a little better
Because I was important
In the life of a child.

Actress Meryl Streep had this reply when asked about the possibility of winning a third Oscar: "I'd rather be voted mother of the year by my family, because nobody realizes that being a good mother is harder than making a movie. Being a housewife and a mother is much more difficult."

It is not what you do for your children but what you have taught them to do for themselves that will make them successful human beings.

ANN LANDERS
Syndicated columnist

Why can't we build orphanages next to homes for the elderly? If someone's sitting in a rocker, it won't be long before a kid will be in their lap.

CLORIS LEACHMAN
Actress

◊ ◊ ◊ FEAR

We cannot escape fear. We can only transform it into a companion that accompanies us on all our exciting adventures . . . . Take a risk a day—one small or bold stroke that will make you feel great once you have done it.

SUSAN JEFFERS
Feel the Fear and Do It Anyway
Fawcett

CENTURIES AGO when mapmakers ran out of the known world before they ran out of parchment, they would sketch a dragon at the edge of the scroll. This was a sign to the explorer that he would be entering unknown territory at his own risk. Unfortunately, some explorers took this symbol literally and were afraid to push on to new worlds. Other more adventurous explorers saw the dragons as a sign of opportunity, a door to virgin territory.

Each of us has a mental map of the world in our heads that contains the information we use to guide ourselves in our day-to-day encounters. Like the maps of long ago, our mental maps also have dragons on them. These represent things that, for whatever reason, we don't want to do or push beyond. It could be a fear of public speaking. It could be a fear of going to a party where we don't know any of the people. It could be a reluctance to participate in a particular sport. Sometimes these dragons are valid. Sometimes, however, they prevent us from discovering something new.

ROGER VON OECH
A Kick in the Seat of the Pants
HarperCollins

A sage once said that if an ocean liner could think and feel, it would never leave its dock; it would be afraid of the thousands of huge waves it would encounter. It would fear all its dangers at once, even though it had to meet them only one wave at a time.

It is very much better sometimes to have a panic feeling beforehand, and then be quite calm when things happen, than to be extremely calm beforehand and to get into a panic when things happen.

WINSTON CHURCHILL (1874-1965)
British prime minister

OUR DEEPEST FEAR is not that we are inadequate. Our deepest fear is that we are powerful beyond measure. It is our light, not our darkness, that most frightens us.

We ask ourselves, who am I to be brilliant, gorgeous, talented, and fabulous? Actually, who are you not to be? You are a child of God. Your playing small doesn't serve the world. There is nothing enlightened about shrinking so that other people won't feel insecure around you.

We are born to make manifest the Glory of God that is within us. It's not just in some of us, it's in everyone, and as we let our own light shine, we consciously give other people permission to do the same. As we are liberated from our own fear, our presence automatically liberates others.

NELSON MANDELA
President of South Africa

❖ ❖ ❖ FOCUS

GOLF GREAT BEN HOGAN stood over a crucial putt. Suddenly a loud train whistle blared in the distance.

After sinking the putt, Hogan was asked if the train whistle bothered him.

"What whistle?" Hogan replied.

I think the one lesson I have learned is that there is no substitute for paying attention.

DIANE SAWYER
Television journalist

❖ ❖ ❖ FORGIVENESS

Those who cannot forgive others break the bridge over which they themselves must pass.

CONFUCIUS (551-479 B.C.)
Chinese philosopher

A WOMAN is dying of AIDS. A priest is summoned. He attempts to comfort her, but to no avail.

"I am lost," she said. "I have ruined my life and every life around me. Now I'm going painfully to hell. There is no hope for me."

The priest saw a framed picture of a pretty girl on the dresser. "Who is this?" he asked. The woman brightened. "She's my daughter, the one beautiful thing in my life."

"And would you help her if she was in trouble, or made a mistake? Would you forgive her? Would you still love her?"

"Of course I would!" cried the woman. "I would do anything for her! Why do you ask such a question?"

"Because I want you to know," said the priest, "that God has a picture of you on His dresser."

The Jokesmith

One of the secrets of a long and fruitful life is to forgive everybody everything every night before you go to bed.

ANN LANDERS
Syndicated columnist

Forgiveness is a funny thing. It warms the heart and cools the sting.

It's better to forgive and forget than to resent and remember.

"Forgiveness," said Epictetus, "is better than revenge, for forgiveness is the sign of a gentle nature, but revenge is the sign of a savage nature."

FRIENDSHIP ❖ ❖ ❖

Make a present and give it to yourself. Make a friend.

A friend is somebody you can be quiet with.

Lots of people want to ride with you in the limo, but what you want is someone who will take the bus with you when the limo breaks down.

OPRAH WINFREY
Television personality

A false friend and a shadow attend only when the sun shines.

BENJAMIN FRANKLIN (1706-1790)
Statesman, scientist, and writer

Friendship is like money, easier made than kept.

SAMUEL BUTLER (1612-1680)
English writer

If you want long friendships, develop a short memory.

Trouble is a sieve through which we sift all our acquaintances. Those too big to go through are our real friends.

ONCE A RICH MAN said he would divide his fortune among his friends, if only he knew who they were.

Years passed and the man died during a mid-winter blizzard. His last request was that his funeral be held at 4 o'clock in the morning.

Although scores had boasted of being his intimate friend,

only three men and one woman turned out to stand sadly beside his grave.

When the will was read, it directed that his estate be divided equally among those who attended his funeral.

Friendship between two persons depends upon the patience of one.

The eye of a friend is a good looking-glass.

FOR A GOOD 15 minutes, the three men at lunch had gone after a mutual acquaintance hammer and tongs, cutting him to ribbons. Finally there were a few seconds of silence as they rested their claws. Then one of them sighed, "I tell you, he's a real menace. You don't know that man like I do."

"Oh, yes, I do," countered another. "I know him every bit as well as you do."

"Nuts," snorted the first man. "How could you possibly know him as well as I do? I'm his best friend."

I always felt that the great high privilege, relief, and comfort of friendship was that one had to explain nothing.

KATHERINE MANSFIELD (1888-1923)
British writer

A real friend is a person who, when you've made a fool of yourself, lets you forget it.

◊ ◊ ◊ **FUN**

Business should be fun. Without fun, people are left wearing emotional raincoats most of their working lives. Building fun into business is vital; it brings life into our daily being. Fun is a powerful motive for most of our activities and should be a direct part of our livelihood. We should not relegate it to something we buy after work with the money we earn.

MICHAEL PHILLIPS and SALLI RASBERRY
Honest Business
Random House

TV PERSONALITY HUGH DOWNS is one of those who believes that if you don't find happiness in your work, you're not going to find it at all.

"The most creative people I know, and some of the happiest, are those who constantly mix business and pleasure," says Downs. "I struggled with the business of broadcasting for at least a dozen years in dead seriousness. I made neither a name nor any money in it until I started having fun with it. I can't say that the change in attitude was the result of any conscious effort on my part, at least not in the way of a plan. It came, rather, from seeing broadcasting as a demanding business that had driven several colleagues to drink and a premature death. I realized that I wanted to avoid that and that I was free to bail out of the business and do something else.

"After having decided to quit, I found that I didn't have to take broadcasting so seriously and began to have fun with it. I have never since decided not to quit, but have left it open. That's the way it should be with any trade or profession."

FUTURE ❖ ❖ ❖

My interest is in the future because I am going to spend the rest of my life there.

CHARLES F. KETTERING (1876-1958)
Inventor

The future is called "perhaps."

TENNESSEE WILLIAMS (1911-1983)
Playwright

When I look into the future, it's so bright, it burns my eyes.

OPRAH WINFREY
Television personality

GIVING ❖ ❖ ❖

Those who do more than is asked of them are never depleted. Only those who fear to give are weakened by giving. The art of giving is entirely a spiritual affair. In this sense, to give one's all is meaningless or there is no bottom where true giving is concerned.

HENRY MILLER
Big Sur and The Oranges of Hieronymus Bosch
New Directions

You get more than you give when you give more than you get.

EPITAPH AT THE GRAVE of Christopher Chapman in Westminster Abbey, bearing the date 1680:

> What I gave, I have,
> What I spent, I had,
> What I left, I lost
> By not giving it.

A MAN WALKED into a packaging and shipping store to have a Christmas present sent out.

When it came time to pay the bill, he complained, "You're charging me more for shipping than I paid for the gift."

The attendant slyly replied, "Maybe you should buy more expensive gifts."

Life is the first gift, love is the second, and understanding is the third.

MARGE PIERCY
Writer

If you have much, give of your wealth; if you have little, give of your heart.

Happiness comes from spiritual wealth, not material wealth . . . . Happiness comes from giving, not getting. If we try hard to bring happiness to others, we cannot stop it from coming to us also. To get joy, we must give it, and to keep joy, we must scatter it.

JOHN TEMPLETON
British investment counselor

AN OLD MAN got on a bus one February 14 carrying a dozen red roses. He sat beside a young man. The young man looked at the roses and said, "Somebody's going to get a beautiful Valentine's Day gift."

"Yes," said the old man.

A few minutes went by and the old man noticed that his young companion was staring at the roses. "Do you have a girl-friend?" the old man asked.

"I do," said the young man. "I'm going to see her now. I'm taking her this." He held up a Valentine's Day card.

They rode along in silence for another 10 minutes, and the old man rose to get off the bus. As he stepped out into the aisle, he suddenly placed the roses on the young man's lap and said, "I think my wife would want you to have these. I'll tell her that I gave them to you."

He left the bus quickly, and as the bus pulled away, the young man turned to see the old man enter the gates of a cemetery.

GOALS ❖ ❖ ❖

*In life there are no **overachievers**—only **underestimators**.*

RICH RUFFALO
Motivational speaker

AT WILLIAMS COLLEGE in Williamstown, Massachusetts, there's a plaque that reads:

Aim high, aim far
Your goal the sky
Your aim the stars.

Shoot for the moon. Even if you miss you'll be among the stars.

As you wander through life, may this always be your goal: Keep your eye on the doughnut and not on the hole.

As long as you're going to think anyway—you might as well think BIG!

DONALD TRUMP
Business executive

If you want to be happy, set a goal that commands your thoughts, liberates your energy, and inspires your hopes.

ANDREW CARNEGIE (1835-1919)
Industrialist

The distance a person goes is not as important as the direction.

❖ ❖ ❖ GOLDEN RULE

Practicing the Golden Rule is not a sacrifice, it's an investment.

BYLLYE AVERY
Founder, National Black Women's Health Project

Commit the Golden Rule to life, not just to memory.

GOLF ♦ ♦ ♦

A DOCTOR who had recently done an artificial heart transplant was reassuring the recipient's wife that her husband would soon be well enough to play golf.

The wife replied, "Hasn't the man suffered enough?"

Golf has taught me there is a connection between pain and pleasure. Golf spelled backwards is "flog."

PHYLLIS DILLER
Comedian

They were looking for famous golf sayings to be inscribed in a specified area in the Golf Hall of Fame when it was under construction in Pinehurst, North Carolina. The first one selected is one of the most often-used expressions the game has produced. It's "Oh, no!"

We blame fate for other accidents, but we feel personally responsible when we make a hole in one.

FOR SEVERAL YEARS a lawyer and a doctor had regularly played golf together. They were evenly matched, and there was a keen sense of rivalry.

Then one spring, the lawyer's game suddenly improved so much that the doctor was losing regularly. The doctor's efforts to improve his own game were unsuccessful, but finally he came up with an idea. At a bookstore he picked out three how-to-play golf texts and sent them to the lawyer for a birthday present.

It wasn't long before they were evenly matched again.

❖ ❖ ❖ GOVERNMENT

Democracy is the worst system ever invented—except for all the rest.

> WINSTON CHURCHILL (1874-1965)
> British prime minister

I don't make jokes; I just watch the government and report the facts.

> WILL ROGERS (1879-1935)
> Humorist

The essence of good government is to persuade an impatient nation to accept short-term pains for long-term gains.

MOSES WAS FLEEING from the Egyptians with the Israelites when he came to the Red Sea. He asked God for help and was told that there was good news and bad news.

"The good news," said the voice from on high, "is that I will part the sea so that you and your people can escape."

"And the bad news?" asked Moses.

"You will have to file an environmental impact statement."

> *Dickson's Joke Treasury*
> John Wiley & Sons

WHEN THOMAS JEFFERSON presented his credentials as U.S. minister to France, the French premier remarked, "I see that you have

83

come to replace Benjamin Franklin."

"I have come to succeed him," corrected Jefferson. "No one can replace him."

GRATITUDE ❖ ❖ ❖

I LOOK BACK UPON my youth and realize how so many people gave me help, understanding, courage—very important things to me—and they never knew it. They entered into my life and became powers within me.

All of us live spiritually by what others have given us, often unwittingly, in the significant hours of our life. At the time these significant hours may not even be perceived. We may not recognize them until years later when we look back, as one remembers some long-ago music or a boyhood landscape.

We all owe to others much of the gentleness and wisdom that we have made our own; and we may well ask ourselves what will others owe to us.

ALBERT SCHWEITZER (1875-1965)
French medical missionary

Gratitude is something of which none of us can give too much. For on the smiles, the thanks we give, our little gestures of appreciation, our neighbors build up their philosophy of life.

A POOR SCOTTISH FARMER was out walking one day when he heard a plaintive cry for help coming from a nearby bog. He ran to assist and found a boy mired almost to the waist in the black muck. Extending his staff, the farmer pulled the boy out.

The next day, a handsome team and carriage came up to the Scotsman's small hut, and an elegantly dressed gentleman stepped out. He offered a reward to the Scotsman, who refused it.

Just then the farmer's young son came to the door. Seeing him, the nobleman made the Scotsman an offer: "Let me take your son and give him a good education. If the lad is anything like his father, he'll grow into a man you can be proud of." The Scotsman liked this and shook hands on the bargain.

In time, the Scotsman's son graduated from St. Mary's Hospital Medical School, London. He later became Sir Alexander Fleming, the noted discoverer of penicillin.

Years later the nobleman's son was stricken with pneumonia, but was saved through the use of penicillin. The nobleman was Lord Randolph Churchill, and the son was Winston Churchill.

❖ ❖ ❖ GREATNESS

Unless you choose to do great things with it, it makes no difference how much you are rewarded, or how much power you have.

OPRAH WINFREY
Television personality

Great souls have wills; feeble ones have only wishes.

CHINESE PROVERB

BENJAMIN FRANKLIN BELIEVED that the measure of a person's greatness was the person's goodness. He did not believe one could exist without the other. In 1729, in the *American Weekly Mercury*, Franklin wrote:

"If we were as industrious to become good as to make ourselves great, we should become really great by being good, and the number of valuable people would be much increased.

"But it is a grand mistake to think of being great without goodness; and I pronounce it as certain, that there was never yet a truly great person who was not at the same time truly virtuous."

If you add a little to a little and do this often, soon that little will become great.

HESIOD (8th Century B.C.)
Greek poet

Great minds discuss ideas,
average minds discuss events,
small minds discuss people.

ADMIRAL HYMAN RICKOVER (1900-1986)
U.S. Navy

The really great person is the person who makes every person feel great.

G.K. CHESTERTON (1874-1936)
English writer

HABIT ❖ ❖ ❖

Habit starts out as a thread. As new threads are added, it becomes a rope we cannot break.

A RIDDLE

I AM YOUR constant companion.

I am your greatest helper or heaviest burden.

I will push you onward or drag you down to failure.

I am completely at your command.

Half the things you do might just as well be turned over to me and I will be able to do them quickly and correctly.

I am easily managed—you must merely be firm with me. Show me exactly how you want something done and after a few lessons I will do it automatically.

I am the servant of all great people and, alas, of all failures, as well.

Those who are great, I have made great.

Those who are failures, I have made failures.

I am not a machine, though I work with all the precision of a machine plus the intelligence of a person. You may run me for profit or run me for ruin—it makes no difference to me.

Take me, train me, be firm with me, and I will place the world at your feet. Be easy with me and I will destroy you.

Who am I?

I am habit!

DEFINITION

In•san•i•ty, *n.* Doing the same thing over and over while expecting a different result.

It's easy to tell one lie or have one peanut. The problem is that each leads to another.

HAPPINESS ✦ ✦ ✦

Success is when you get what you want.
Happiness is when you want what you get.

The three grand essentials of happiness are: something to do, someone to love, and something to hope for.

ALEXANDER CHALMERS (1759-1834)
British writer

Those who bring sunshine to the lives of others cannot keep it from themselves.

J.M. BARRIE (1860-1937)
Scottish writer

THOUGH: :ative people, people who try, who care,
people wl. ed pay a price—but the rewards are inde-
scribable. It 1 /ards which are returned from respect for
one's own valu own way of living—in trying to be incor-
ruptible, at least in 1g not to be corrupted. The state of inter-
nal contentment we c. l happiness means using the resources of
the mind and the heart—as deeply and fully as you can.

LEO ROSTEN (1908-1997)
Writer

OF ALL THOSE who have tried, down the ages, to outline a program for happiness, few have succeeded as well as William Henry Channing, a clergyman who was chaplain to the U.S. Senate in the middle of the last century. He put it this way:

> "To live content with small means, to seek elegance rather than luxury, and refinement rather than fashion; to be worthy, not respectable, and wealthy, not rich; to study hard, think quietly, talk gently, act frankly; to listen to the stars and birds, to babes and sages, with open heart; to bear all cheerfully, do all bravely, await occasion, hurry never; in a word, to let the spiritual, unbidden and unconscious, grow up through the common. This is to be my symphony."

Not what you have, but what you see;
Not what you see, but what you choose;
Not what seems fair, but what is true;
Not what you dream, but what you do;
Not what you take, but what you give;
Not as you pray, but as you live.

These are the things that mar or bless
The sum of human happiness.

My creed is that:

Happiness is the only good.
The place to be happy is here.
The time to be happy is now.
The way to be happy is to make others so.

ROBERT G. INGERSOLL (1833-1899)
Writer and orator

Happiness is not a state to arrive at, but a manner of traveling.

Happiness is like a butterfly. The more you chase it, the more it will elude you. But if you turn your attention to other things, it comes and softly sits on your shoulder.

Not what we have, but what we enjoy, constitutes our abundance.

There's no time like the pleasant.

OLIVER HERFORD
Humorist

NINE ESSENTIALS for a full and contented life:
Health enough to make work a pleasure.
Wealth enough to support your needs.
Strength to battle with difficulties and overcome them.
Grace enough to confess your sins and forsake them.
Patience enough to toil until some good is accomplished.
Charity enough to see some good in your neighbor.
Love enough to move you to be useful and helpful to others.
Faith enough to make real the things of God.
Hope enough to remove all anxious fears concerning the future.

JOHANN WOLFGANG VON GOETHE (1749-1832)
German writer

Perfectionists are never perfectly happy.

TOO MANY FRIENDSHIPS languish at the bottom of our priority list, untouched like some endlessly postponed dessert. Too many marriages grow numb waiting for intimate stretches of time. Too few of us resolve to sing, or to walk in the snow, to make love, or to make someone laugh. Too many of us forget what we want.

The pursuit of happiness that once carried the weight of the American Revolution now seems frivolous and has to wait. But joy is also a habit. Use it or lose it. And happiness is not a banal smiley face to stick on an envelope. It's an option that we must exercise or watch atrophy.

ELLEN GOODMAN
Journalist

◊ ◊ ◊ **HEALTH**

THE MURDER OF GRABWELL GROMMET

by Arthur Hoppe

ON THE MORNING of his 42nd birthday, Grabwell Grommet awoke to the peal of particularly ominous thunder. Glancing out the window with bleary eyes, he saw written in fiery letters across the sky:

"SOMEONE IS TRYING TO KILL YOU, GRABWELL GROMMET."

With shaking hands, Grommet lit his first cigarette of the day. He didn't question the message. You don't question messages like that. His only question was, "Who?"

At breakfast, as he salted his fried eggs, he told his wife, Gratia, "Someone is trying to kill me."

"Who?" she asked with horror.

Grommet slowly stirred the cream and sugar into his coffee and shook his head. "I don't know," he said.

Convinced though he was, Grommet couldn't go to the police with such a story. He decided his only course of action was to go about his daily routine and hope somehow to outwit his would-be murderer.

He tried to think on the drive to the office. But the frustrations of making time by beating lights and switching lanes occupied him wholly. Nor, once behind his desk, could he find a moment what with jangling phones, urgent memos, and the problems and decisions piling up as they did each day.

It wasn't until his second martini at lunch that the full terror of his position struck him. It was all he could do to finish his lasagna Milanese.

"I can't panic," he said to himself, lighting up his cigar. "I simply must live my life as usual."

So he worked till seven as usual. Drove home fast as usual. Had his two cocktails as usual. Studied business reports as usual. And took his usual two sleeping pills in order to get his usual six hours of sleep.

As the days passed, he manfully stuck to his routine. And as the months went by, he began to take a perverse pleasure in his ability to survive.

"Whoever's trying to get me," he'd say proudly to his wife, "hasn't got me yet. I'm too smart for him."

"Oh, please be careful," she'd reply, ladling him a second helping of beef Stroganoff.

The pride grew as he managed to go on living for years. But, as it must to all men, death came at last to Grabwell Grommet. It came at his desk on a particularly busy day. He was 53.

His grief-stricken widow demanded a full autopsy.

But it showed only emphysema, arteriosclerosis, duodenal ulcers, cirrhosis of the liver, cardiac necrosis, a cerebrovascular aneurysm, pulmonary edema, obesity, circulatory insufficiency, and a touch of lung cancer.

"How glad Grabwell would have been to know," said the widow smiling proudly through her tears, "that he died of natural causes."

———————

Advice for executives over 50: Keep an open mind and a closed refrigerator.

———————

If you can swallow a pill while drinking from a water fountain, you deserve to get well.

———————

If you want to be the picture of health, make sure you have a happy frame of mind.

◆ ◆ ◆ **HEROES**

We can't all be heroes because someone has to sit on the curb and clap as they go by.

WILL ROGERS (1879-1935)
Humorist

———————

LET IT NEVER be forgotten that glamour is not greatness; applause is not fame; prominence is not eminence. The man of the hour is not apt to be the man of the ages. A stone may sparkle, but that does not make it a diamond; people may have money, but that does not make them a success.

It is what the unimportant people do that really counts and determines the course of history. The greatest forces in the universe are never spectacular. Summer showers are more effective than hurricanes, but they get no publicity. The world would soon

93

die but for the fidelity, loyalty, and consecration of those whose names are unhonored and unsung.

JAMES R. SIZOO

HINDSIGHT ❖ ❖ ❖

The only perfect science is hindsight.

After the ship has sunk, everyone knows how she might have been saved.

ITALIAN PROVERB

Our lives would run a lot more smoothly if second thoughts came first.

HISTORY ❖ ❖ ❖

CHARLES A. BEARD, the historian, was once asked if he could summarize the lessons of history. Beard replied that he could do it with four simple observations:

1. Whom the gods would destroy they first make mad with power.
2. The mills of the gods grind slowly, but they grind exceedingly fine.
3. The bee fertilizes the flower it robs.
4. When it is dark enough, you can see the stars.

I don't subscribe to the thesis, "Let the buyer beware." I prefer the disregarded one that goes, "Let the seller be honest."

ISAAC ASIMOV (1920-1992)
Writer

Honesty is like an icicle; once it melts, that's the end of it.

A man who had spent a fruitless day fishing picked out three fat fish in the market. "Before you wrap them," he said to the store manager, "toss them to me, one by one. That way I'll be able to tell my wife I caught them, and I'll be speaking the truth."

You can fool some of the people all of the time, and all of the people some of the time; but you can't fool all of the people all of the time.

ABRAHAM LINCOLN (1809-1865)
16th President of the U.S.

❖ ❖ ❖ HOPE

*Hope looks for the good in people
    instead of harping on the worst.*

*Hope opens doors where despair
    closes them.*

*Hope discovers what can be done instead
    of grumbling about what cannot.*

95

Hope draws its power from a deep trust
in God and the basic goodness of human nature.

Hope "lights a candle" instead of "cursing
the darkness."

Hope regards problems, small or large,
as opportunities.

Hope cherishes no illusions, nor does it
yield to cynicism.

Hope sets big goals and is not frustrated
by repeated difficulties or setbacks.

Hope pushes ahead when it would be easy
to quit.

Hope puts up with modest gains, realizing
that "the longest journey starts with one step."

Hope accepts misunderstanding as the
price for serving the greater good of others.

Hope is a good loser because it has the
divine assurance of final victory.

FATHER JAMES KELLER (1900-1977)
Founder, The Christophers

———————

There are no hopeless situations—only people who are hopeless about them.

DINAH SHORE (1917-1994)
Entertainer

———————

❖ ❖ ❖ HUMAN NATURE

One of the most tragic things I know about human nature is that all of us tend to put off living. We are all dreaming of some magical rose garden over the horizon—instead of enjoying the roses that are blooming outside our windows today.

DALE CARNEGIE (1888-1955)
Writer and speaker

It's easy to be an angel when nobody ruffles your feathers.

A PREACHER put this question to a class of children: "If all the good people in the world were red and all the bad people were green, what color would you be?"

Little Linda Jean thought mightily for a moment. Then her face brightened and she replied: "Reverend, I'd be streaky!"

ERNEST KURTZ
The Spirituality of Imperfection
Bantam Books

That old law about "an eye for an eye" leaves everybody blind.

MARTIN LUTHER KING, JR. (1929-1968)
Civil rights leader

There are many more people trying to meet the right person than to become the right person.

GLORIA STEINEM
Feminist and writer

97

As a rule,
Man's a fool.
When it's hot,
He wants it cool,
And when it's cool,
He wants it hot,
Always wanting
What is not.

Who gossips to you will gossip of you.

TURKISH PROVERB

There are two insults people won't endure: the assertion that they have no sense of humor and the doubly impertinent assertion that they have never known trouble.

SINCLAIR LEWIS (1885-1951)
Writer

HUMAN RELATIONS ❖ ❖ ❖

HERE ARE FIVE simple suggestions for getting along better with people:

1. Never miss a chance to say a kind or encouraging word to or about somebody. Praise good work, no matter who does it.

2. When you make a promise, honor it. Just don't make too many.

3. Hold your tongue. Always say less than you think. Speak softly and persuasively. How you say something often means more than what you say.

4. Express an interest in others—in their pursuits, their work, and their families. Have fun with those who rejoice. Offer consolation to those who mourn a loss. Let everyone you meet feel that you regard him or her as an important individual.

5. Be cheerful. Don't depress others by complaining about your small problems and disappointments. Remember, everyone has some burden to carry.

People who fight fire with fire usually end up with ashes.

ABIGAIL VAN BUREN
Syndicated columnist

To be popular, be both tactful and truthful.

The first thing to learn in dealing with others is noninterference with their own particular ways of being happy, provided those ways do not assume to interfere with ours.

WILLIAM JAMES (1842-1910)
Philosopher and psychologist

The only way to live happily with people is to overlook their faults and admire their virtues.

The biggest step you can take is the one you take when you meet the other person halfway.

If you want to be well-liked by others, don't set out to make yourself liked. You will only be thinking of yourself that way. Instead, develop a sincere and genuine interest in the other fellow and being liked will follow naturally.

The wisest man I have ever known once said to me: "Nine out of 10 people improve on acquaintance," and I have found his words true.

FRANK SWINNERTON

Someone has to give way. There is a rule in sailing that the more maneuverable ship should give way to the less maneuverable craft. I think this is sometimes a good rule to follow in human relationships as well.

DR. JOYCE BROTHERS
Psychologist

Enemies are made, not born.

HUMILITY ❖ ❖ ❖

Modesty is the art of drawing attention to whatever it is you are being humble about.

If you think you are too small to do big things, try doing small things in a big way.

100

❖ ❖ ❖ HUMOR

Laughter is an instant vacation.

MILTON BERLE
Comedian

A sense of humor is the pole that adds balance to our steps as we walk the tightrope of life.

It's a big person who can laugh at oneself with others and enjoy it as much as they do.

❖ ❖ ❖ IDEAS

Getting a great idea is like sitting on a sharp tack—it makes you jump up and do something!

The thoughts of two people are more valuable than money. When two people exchange dollar bills, each still has only one dollar. When they exchange ideas, each then has two ideas.

To stay ahead, you must have your next idea waiting in the wings.

ROSABETH MOSS KANTER
Educator, business consultant, and writer

Man's mind stretched by a new idea never goes back to its original dimensions.

OLIVER WENDELL HOLMES (1809-1894)
Physician and writer

The thoughts that come often unsought, and, as it were, drop into the mind, are commonly the most valuable of any we have.

JOHN LOCKE (1632-1704)
English philosopher

YOU MAY TREAT IDEAS as bullets or seeds. You may shoot ideas or you may sow them. You may hit people on the head with them, or you plant them in their hearts.

Use them as bullets, and they kill inspiration and neutralize motivation. Use them as seeds, they take root, grow, and become a reality in the life in which they are planted. The only risk taken when seeds are planted is that they become a part of the one in whom they grow. The originator will probably get no credit for the idea. If one is willing not to get credit for an idea, a rich harvest will be reaped.

"It is more blessed to give than to receive."

RICHARD HALVERSON

BACK IN 1820, the average person in England wrote only three letters a year. And with good reason. Letters in those days were mailed without a cover and could be read by anyone.

But William Mulready had an idea to ensure privacy—the envelope. On a visit to France, Mulready noticed that messages from an important person often were completely enclosed in "a little paper case . . . impervious to the peering eyes of the curious."

The idea of sending letters shielded from curious eyes was an instant success. The volume of letters handled by the British postal service soared beyond anyone's expectations.

Today, there are billions of Mulready's little paper envelopes safely traveling around the world.

Ideas, like fleas, jump from person to person. Unlike fleas, they don't bite everyone.

IN 1901, H.C. Booth was sitting in a rocking chair on his front porch, watching the sun set. Living in the Midwest, he was also watching the dust blow.

As he contemplated the scene, he wondered, "What if we could reverse the wind? Then instead of blowing dust, we could pull dust."

Later that year, he invented the vacuum cleaner.

ED AGRESTA
Don't Count the Days, Make the Days Count

❖ ❖ ❖ IMAGINATION

TWO ELDERLY MEN shared a room at a nursing home. The one near the window was suffering from a weakened heart, having had a series of heart attacks. The other man had fallen and broken his hip. Both were confined to bed, unable to get up and walk around to relieve the tedium and monotony of their situations.

Every now and then, when both were awake, the man near the window would look out and describe what was going on.

Since they were on the second floor, the other man, with the broken hip, could see only the sky.

"The park is beautiful," the one would say, then go on to describe the people walking there. One day he began to tell about a lovely young nurse who seemed to walk through the park at the same time each day. "She's lovely," he would say, "so young, so alive, I wish you could see her."

This went on for several days, when finally the man near the window noticed that a young intern seemed to be coming from the opposite direction from the nurse at the same time each day. They did not know each other and the first few days only nodded as they passed. But, then, the man said, they began to stop briefly for a chat. Before long it had blossomed into a romance and they began meeting there on a bench, catching 10 or 15 minutes together before going on to their appointed duties.

The man would also describe the beauty of the park—the green grass, the spring flowers, the tall shady trees. The man by the window painted the picture as best he could for his companion. Then one night, abruptly, he died, the victim of a final heart attack.

A few days after the funeral the other elderly man asked the nurses if he might be moved to the window bed. He missed so much not knowing what was going on in the park below.

That evening, late, his wish was granted and he was moved to the other bed. The hip was mending slowly, but now he could be raised to get a good view of the park and all the lovely sights his friend had described. He could hardly wait for the next morning when he would be able to look out, and he was especially eager to see the young nurse and her intern.

At the crack of dawn the next morning, he raised himself on one elbow and looked out the window. There was nothing there but a dreary asphalt-covered parking lot.

If you live your life out of memory, you live out of your history. That's what once was. If you live out of your imagination, you live out of your potential. That's what can be.

Imagination lit every lamp in this country, built every church, performed every act of kindness and progress, created more and better things for more people. It is the priceless ingredient for a better day.

HENRY J. TAYLOR (1856-1941)
Historian

MILLIONS OF PEOPLE have either read Frank Baum's *The Wizard of Oz* or seen it on TV—or both. Yet it's a safe bet that few people know where the name "Oz" came from.

According to the late author's autobiography, he had outlined the story of Dorothy and the Tin Man and the Straw Man and the Cowardly Lion and all the others in his mind, but still had not hit upon a name for the magic land they were seeking, when his eyes fell on a filing cabinet in a corner of his office.

The top drawer of this file was labeled "A-H," the second drawer, "I-N," and the bottom drawer, "O-Z." "That's it!" he cried delightedly. "OZ!"

❖ ❖ ❖ IMPROVEMENT

A CHIEF STUMBLING BLOCK in the way of success is success itself. The moment a manager decides he is successful enough or smart enough to "rest on his laurels," he shifts into reverse. The choice is clear. You either plod forward, or you slide backwards.

Savvy companies and savvy managers know this very well.

105

They're never satisfied. They never stop trailing perfection.

The story is told of the New York agency that dreamed up a famous ad for a famous car. It read: "At 60 m.p.h. the loudest noise in the new Rolls-Royce comes from the electric clock."

With great pride an agency adman showed this creation to a visiting Rolls-Royce executive. Instead of elation, the executive displayed a worried frown.

"We'll have to do something about that clock," he replied.

Amusing story. But it makes a potent point. Dissatisfaction. The savvy manager's constant quest for self-improvement.

ROBERT E. LEVINSON
Super Savvy!
Garrett Publishing

IT'S INTERESTING TO NOTE that the gold medal winners are not necessarily the most talented athletes in their event or even the ones that trained the hardest. In most cases, what separates them from the rest is that they trained *smarter*.

It's the same outside of sports too. People who work harder often lose out to those who know how to work smarter.

Working smarter is a more sophisticated concept than working harder. To discover the key ingredient to working smarter, take the following quiz:

There are four steel rings. One steel ring can hold a maximum of 80 pounds. The second ring can hold no more than 60 pounds. The third can hold a maximum of 40 pounds and the fourth, 20 pounds. If any of the rings has to support more than its maximum, it will break. Now if these four rings are linked together, what is the greatest weight that the entire chain link can support?

a. 200 pounds
b. 100 pounds

c. 80 pounds

d. 20 pounds

e. none of the above

Hint: A chain is only as strong as its weakest link.

Answer: d. 20 pounds

Before you start thinking you're preparing for a college entrance exam, here's the point . . . .

The only way to strengthen the *entire* chain link is to strengthen its weakest link since the maximum amount of weight the chain will hold will always be limited by its *weakest* link.

And it's the same with you and me. We are limited most in life by our weakest links—our greatest weaknesses. The quickest, smartest, and most effective way for us to improve is to build up our weak points.

Quite obvious? Sure. But isn't it human nature to focus our energies on the things that we do best and ignore our shortcomings? No one likes to confront their deficiencies.

The greatest rule to making *significant* improvements in ourselves is to spend more time strengthening our weaknesses than we do polishing our strengths. Once we start investing our time this way we are working smarter. And we will profit by the rewards of improved performance and the personal satisfaction that goes with it.

ROB GILBERT
Editor, *Bits & Pieces*

See everything.

Overlook a great deal.

Improve a little.

POPE JOHN XXIII

When someone is no longer eager to do better, that person is done for.

Every little bit helps.

Every little quit hurts.

IF YOU START your day with these four questions, you'll make every day a more productive day . . . .

1. What's the best thing that can happen today?
2. What's the worst thing that can happen today?
3. What can I do today to make sure that the best thing does happen?
4. What can I do today to make sure that the worst thing doesn't happen?

THE GENERAL MANAGER of a small company was extremely popular. He was also a very effective executive. When he retired, the company gave a special dinner in his honor.

When he rose to thank people for the occasion, somebody asked him, "Joe, what was your secret for handling people?"

"I didn't have any secret," said Joe. "I think the important thing was that I realized I had a lot to learn. I kept trying to learn to deal with people more effectively from my first day till my last.

"When I discovered that something worked well in handling people, I made a note of it and tried to make it a habit. When something got me in trouble—or produced undesirable results—I made a note of that too. Gradually, believe it or not, I began to learn. Over the years it began to add up. I still make plenty of mistakes, but they're not as frequent as they used to be."

Joe's self-improvement system requires three fundamentals. One is to start with the realization that you are far from perfect. The second is to stay alert, to watch what works and what doesn't work and remember it. The third is to want to improve badly enough to keep putting the constructive ideas to work until they become a habit.

❖ ❖ ❖ INGENUITY

A LITTLE GIRL was sent upstairs by her father to empty the wastebaskets, but she returned so quickly that her father said: "You couldn't have emptied all the baskets in this time."

"They didn't need emptying, Dad," the child replied. "They just needed stepping in."

AN ARCHITECT built a cluster of office buildings around a central green. When construction was completed, the landscape crew asked him where he wanted the sidewalks. "Just plant the grass solidly between the buildings," was his reply.

By late summer the new lawn was laced with paths of trodden grass between the buildings. These paths turned in easy curves and were sized according to traffic flow.

In the fall, the architect simply paved the paths. Not only did the paths have a design beauty, they responded directly to user needs.

❖ ❖ ❖ INGRATITUDE

AN ELDERLY WOMAN was taking care of her three-year-old grandson one day. They went to the beach, and as the child made sand castles, the grandmother dozed off.

As she slept, a huge wave dragged the child out to sea. When she awoke, she was devastated. She fell on her knees and prayed. "God, if You save my grandson, I promise I'll make it up to You. I'll join whatever club You want me to. I'll volunteer up at the hospital. I'll give to the poor and do anything else You ask."

Suddenly, a huge wave tossed the child back on the beach at her feet. She saw that there was color in his cheeks, and that he was breathing.

He was alive!

She put her hands on her hips, looked skyward, and said sharply, "He had a hat, You know!"

PAUL E. MCGHEE
Health, Healing and the Amuse System
Kendall/Hunt

INITIATIVE ❖ ❖ ❖

SOME YEARS AGO, Steve Wallenda of the Flying Wallendas high-wire circus act learned that his friend Joel Aronsen had to have a heart transplant. He also learned that Joel didn't have the money or insurance coverage to pay for it.

Telling Aronsen, "I'm here to save your life," Wallenda set up a 40-foot high-wire in a parking lot at the Rawhide Amusement Park in Scottsdale, Arizona. Mounting the high wire, Wallenda announced he would stay up there for four days in a fund-raising effort to pay for his friend's operation.

Wallenda didn't wait for anyone to tell him how he could help. He saw the need and pushed his own self-starter button. "Initiative" is what they call it.

110

❖ ❖ ❖ INSPIRATION

Aspire to *inspire* before you *expire.*

PEOPLE ALL OVER the world have participated in Weight Watchers. An interviewer once asked Jean Nidetch, the group's founder, how she had been able to help so many people.

Nidetch replied that as a teenager, she used to walk through a park frequently, and she would observe mothers chatting and watchfully "ignoring" their children as the youngsters sat on swings with no one to push them.

"I'd give them a push," Nidetch said, "and you know what happens when you push kids on a swing? Pretty soon they're pumping, doing it themselves. That's what my role in life is—I'm there to give others a push."

IN 1861, near the beginning of the American Civil War, Julia Ward Howe stood one day watching the Army of the Potomac as the troops hurried from the North to the southern battlefields, singing the rough, popular song, "John Brown's Body."

She was gripped with the desire to write other words for the magnificent rhythmic melody. All that night words and phrases were casting themselves in her mind. Shortly before dawn she wrote the stanzas, then fell into a sound sleep.

Upon publication, the song spread through the land like wildfire. It is said that when Abraham Lincoln heard it for the first time, he broke into tears. The song was "The Battle Hymn of the Republic."

THE YEAR 1741 was perhaps the most depressing in all of George Frideric Handel's lifetime.

His latest opera was pronounced a dismal failure, and his Italian opera company in London was disbanded. Worse still, Queen Caroline had passed away that year, and with her passing, the commissions he received for composing music for royal occasions all but dried up.

He had also suffered a stroke several years earlier. It had left him not only physically drained, but without the spark of genius that had made his music so popular.

Then one day late in the year, Handel received a manuscript from Charles Jennens, a little known poet, along with a request that Handel set it to music. As Handel pored over the lines, a shiver ran down his spine. Somehow Jennens' words had special meaning for him.

At once Handel started putting them to music. He worked through that night and much of the next day. And, in fact, he worked with total fervor for 22 more days, hardly stopping to eat or sleep.

When Handel's composition was complete, he knew at once that it would be the masterpiece he would be remembered for. In the spring of 1742 his *Messiah* was first performed and greeted with critical acclaim.

And what were the words that Jennens had written that took Handel from near despair to the heights of musical inspiration, the words that seemed to be written for him? "He was despised and rejected of men. He looked for someone to have pity on him, but there was no man. He trusted in God. God did not leave his soul in hell. I know that my Redeemer liveth. Rejoice. Hallelujah!"

❖ ❖ ❖ INTEGRITY

SOME TIME AGO, an article in *National Racquetball* magazine told the story of Reuben Gonzales, who was in the final match of a professional racquetball tournament. It was Gonzales' first shot at a victory on the pro circuit, and he was playing the perennial champion.

In the fourth and final game, at match point, Gonzales made a super "kill" shot into the front wall to win it all. The referee called it good. One of the two linesmen affirmed that the shot was in.

But Gonzales, after a moment's hesitation, turned around, shook his opponent's hand, and declared that his shot had "skipped" into the wall, hitting the court floor first. As a result, he lost the match. He walked off the court. Everybody was stunned.

The next issue of *National Racquetball* magazine displayed Reuben Gonzales on its front cover. The story searched for an explanation of this first-ever occurrence on the professional racquetball circuit.

Who could ever imagine it in any sport or endeavor? A player, with everything officially in his favor, with victory in his hand, disqualified *himself* at match point and lost!

When asked why he did it, Reuben said, "It was the only thing I could do to maintain my integrity."

DENIS WAITLEY
Being the Best
Oliver-Nelson

———

IN ORDER TO BE a leader, a man must have followers. And to have followers, a man must have their confidence. Hence the supreme quality for a leader is unquestionably integrity. Without it, no real success is possible, no matter whether it is on a section gang, on a football field, in an army, or in an office.

If a man's associates find him guilty of phoniness, if they find that he lacks forthright integrity, he will fail. His teachings and actions must square with each other. The first great need, therefore, is integrity and high purpose.

DWIGHT D. EISENHOWER (1890-1969)
34th President of the U.S.

Knowing what's right doesn't mean much unless you do what's right.

My basic principle is that you don't make decisions because they are easy, you don't make them because they're cheap, you don't make them because they're popular; you make them because they're right.

THEODORE M. HESBURGH
Former president, The University of Notre Dame

In matters of taste, swim with the current; in matters of principle, stand like a rock.

THOMAS JEFFERSON (1743-1826)
Third President of the U.S.

The straight and narrow path would be wider if more people used it.

KAY INGRAM
Writer

IN 1927, a real estate and insurance company in Savannah, Georgia, failed. Some 500 stockholders in the firm were out several hundred thousand dollars.

Both the owner of the company, a man named Mercer, and his young son vowed that if it were in their power, someday the stockholders would be repaid their losses.

The company was never able to get going again, and some years later the father died. His son, however, never forgot the debt—someday, somehow, he would repay it.

Twenty-eight years later the son deposited a check for $300,000 in a Savannah bank to repay the debt to the stockholders. It had taken a long time for the son to fulfill his father's promise, but finally it was done.

The young man was Johnny Mercer, the songwriter and singer. One of the many popular songs that he wrote, and from which he earned enough in royalties to be able to pay off the debt, was "Accentuate the Positive."

The power of ideals is incalculable. We see no power in a drop of water. But let it get into a crack in a rock and be turned to ice, and it splits the rock; turned into steam, it drives the pistons of the most powerful engines. Something has happened to it that makes active and effective the power that is latent in it.

ALBERT SCHWEITZER (1875-1965)
French medical missionary

THE PRICELESS INGREDIENT

IN THE CITY of Baghdad lived Hakeem, the Wise One, and many people went to him for counsel, which he gave freely to all, asking nothing in return.

There came to him a young man, who had spent much but got little, and said, "Tell me, Wise One, what shall I do to receive the most for that which I spend?"

115

Hakeem answered, "A thing that is bought or sold has no value unless it contains that which cannot be bought or sold. Look for the Priceless Ingredient."

"But, what is the Priceless Ingredient?" asked the young man.

Spoke the Wise One, "My son, the Priceless Ingredient of every product in the marketplace is the Honor and Integrity of him who makes it. Consider his name before you buy."

from a 1921 advertisement for Squibb

THE WORD "integrity" means "a state or quality of being whole, complete, or undivided." People who have integrity are whole, complete, and undivided—they follow through and actually do what they say they will do.

If you don't keep your word, your wholeness and completeness break down, and you become divided. You'll be in a tug-of-war with yourself.

If you want to be known as a person of high integrity, simply have your actions equal your words.

INTELLIGENCE ❖ ❖ ❖

The test of a first-rate intelligence is the ability to hold two opposed ideas in the mind at the same time, and still retain the ability to function.

F. SCOTT FITZGERALD (1896-1940)
Writer

Genius has limits; stupidity does not.

116

❖ ❖ ❖ IRONY

"No, WE HAVEN'T had any in a long time now," said the supermarket clerk to the shopper.

"Whoa!" said a manager who had just come along. "I'm sure we have, ma'am. This is a new clerk, and he doesn't know how we keep our stock records and inventory. We've got plenty in the warehouse and will get some over this afternoon. If you come back after lunch, we'll have all you need. Now, tell me, just what was it that he said we haven't had in a long time?"

"Rain," said the woman.

───

WHILE SHE WAS ENJOYING a transatlantic ocean trip, Billie Burke, the famous actress, noticed that a gentleman at the next table was suffering from a bad cold.

"Are you uncomfortable?" she asked sympathetically. The man nodded.

"I'll tell you just what to do for it," she offered. "Go back to your stateroom and drink lots of orange juice. Take two aspirins. Cover yourself with all the blankets you can find. Sweat the cold out. I know just what I'm talking about. I'm Billie Burke from Hollywood."

The man smiled warmly and introduced himself in return. "Thanks," he said, "I'm Dr. Mayo from the Mayo Clinic."

───

AT CEREMONIES COMMEMORATING the hundredth anniversary of Harry S. Truman's birth, the White House counsel during the Truman Administration was reminiscing. He recalled being at a White House banquet one night when one of the guests turned to the woman seated next to him.

"Did I get your name correctly?" he asked. "Is your name Post?"

117

"Yes, it is," the woman answered.

"Is it Emily Post?"

"Yes," she replied.

"Are you the world-renowned authority on manners?" the man asked.

"Yes," Mrs. Post said. "Why do you ask?"

"Because," the man said, "you have just eaten my salad."

———————

A YOUNG MAN who lived on a mountainside longed to leave home. Every morning he would look out across the valley to a house high on the other side. It had windows of shimmering gold, and he yearned to go there and make his fortune. His parents kept asking him to wait. But one day he could wait no longer, and he left home.

The journey was difficult. The path to the valley floor was blocked by huge boulders and fallen trees. By midday he came to a river and nearly drowned as he forded it. On the other side, the brush was heavy and it tore at his clothes and skin. The way up to the house on the other side was steep.

Exhausted, he was ready to drop in his tracks when he came upon a clearing. He had found the house! Frantically he ran to touch its windows. To his dismay, he found them to be made of ordinary glass.

Dejected, bitter with disappointment, he turned toward home. Suddenly, he caught a glimpse of the house he lived in and he gasped. Its windows were shining like gold!

———————

◆ ◆ ◆ **JOKES**

FABLE HAS IT that Satan challenged Saint Peter to a baseball game.

Saint Peter laughed. "Are you kidding? I've got Babe Ruth, Ty Cobb, Christy Mathewson, and a host of all-time greats. Who have you got?"

Satan snickered. "The umpires."

> JIM BOUTON and ELIOT ASINOF
> *Strike Zone*
> Viking

I just got out of the hospital. I was in a speed-reading accident. I hit a bookmark.

> STEVEN WRIGHT
> Comedian

When people ask me if I have any spare change, I tell them I have it at home in my spare wallet.

> NICK ARNETTE
> Comedian

FRIENDS OF COMEDIAN George Burns always kidded him about his singing. Burns, a master of self-deprecating humor, decided to take advantage of this and insure his voice for a million dollars. He thought it would be a wonderful publicity stunt.

"I was so excited," said Burns, "I couldn't wait to rush down to the insurance company. I took a cassette and a tape recorder with me so the insurance man could hear my voice. It was one of my best numbers—a syncopated version of "Yankee Doodle

119

Blues" with a yodeling finish. The insurance man listened patiently to the whole thing. Then he just looked at me and said, 'Mr. Burns, you should have come to us before you had the accident.'"

Upon accepting an award, comedian Jack Benny once remarked, "I really don't deserve this, but I have arthritis and I don't deserve that either."

Due to the loss of an eye in the Second World War, the Israeli statesman Moshe Dayan had to wear an eyepatch. One day, after being stopped for speeding, he argued with the policeman, "I have only one eye. What do you want me to watch—the speedometer or the road?"

Topol's Treasury of Jewish Humor, Wit and Wisdom
Barricade Books

A YOUNG BUSINESS OWNER was opening a new branch office, and a friend decided to send a floral arrangement for the grand opening.

When the friend arrived at the opening, he was appalled to find that his wreath bore the inscription: "Rest in peace."

Angry, he complained to the florist. After apologizing, the florist said, "Look at it this way—somewhere there's a man buried under a wreath today that says, 'Good luck in your new location.'"

You can observe a lot by watching.

YOGI BERRA
Baseball player

LEO DUROCHER COULD NEEDLE ballplayers and umpires with the best of them when he was a manager in the major leagues. It was a talent he developed as a player. Once when the New York Giants were playing an exhibition game at West Point, a few Cadets were giving Leo the needle as he tossed the ball around the infield. They wanted to know how a runt like him ever made it to the big leagues. Old-timers remember his reply: "My congressman appointed me." ───────────

Entertainer Victor Borge told a friend that he could tell time by his piano. His friend was incredulous, so Borge volunteered to demonstrate. He pounded out a crashing march. Immediately there came a banging on the wall and a shrill voice screamed, "Stop that noise. Don't you know it's 1:30 in the morning?"

❖ ❖ ❖ **JOY**

Real joy comes not from ease or riches or from the praise of others, but from doing something worthwhile.

WILFRED GRENFELL (1865-1940)
English medical missionary

───────────

We often consider that joy is essential. I don't know of any other culture so bent on pleasure. We are lost in the pursuit of pleasure so much that we forget there are other things . . . . Joy is a great teacher, but so is disillusionment . . . to deny yourself any of these is not experiencing life totally.

LEO BUSCAGLIA
Educator and writer

───────────

JUDGMENT ❖ ❖ ❖

One of the most serious mistakes we can make is to confuse the thing we call "intelligence" with another thing called "judgment." The two do not always, or necessarily, go together; many persons of high intelligence have notoriously poor judgment.

SYDNEY J. HARRIS (1917-1986)
Syndicated columnist

WHEN WE PLANT a rose in the earth, we notice that it is small, but we do not criticize it as "rootless and stemless." We treat it as a seed, giving it the water and nourishment required of a seed.

When it first shoots up out of the earth, we don't condemn it as immature and underdeveloped; nor do we criticize the buds for not being open when they appear. We stand in wonder at the process taking place and give the plant the care it needs at each stage of its development.

The rose is a rose from the time it is a seed to the time it dies. Within it, at all times, it contains its whole potential. It seems to be constantly in the process of its whole potential.

It seems to be constantly in the process of change; yet at each state, at each moment, it is perfectly all right as it is.

Do not think of your faults; still less of others' faults; look for what is good and strong; and try to imitate it; your faults will drop off, like dead leaves when their time comes.

JOHN RUSKIN (1819-1900)
English writer

122

One ailment that antibiotics will never stamp out is premature formation of opinion.

You are entitled to your own opinion.
You are not entitled to your own facts.

Human nature seems to endow people with the ability to size up everybody but themselves.

❖ ❖ ❖ **KINDNESS**

Kindness is the inability to remain at ease in the presence of another person who is ill at ease, the inability to remain comfortable in the presence of another who is uncomfortable, the inability to have peace of mind when one's neighbor is troubled.

RABBI SAMUEL H. HOLDENSON
Religious leader

Funny thing about kindness. The more it's used, the more you have of it.

Kindness is the golden chain by which society is bound together.

JOHANN WOLFGANG VON GOETHE (1749-1832)
German writer

"YOU CAN ACCOMPLISH by kindness," wrote Publilius Syrus in the first century B.C., "what you cannot do by force."

William McKinley, President of the United States from 1897 to 1901, understood that principle. During one of his congressional campaigns, before becoming president, he was persistently followed by a reporter from an opposition newspaper. This young man seized every possible opportunity to misrepresent McKinley's views and to hold him up to ridicule.

McKinley took this barrage of unfair criticism with fortitude, and even remarked that at least he could admire the young reporter's determination.

Finally, however, the future president's admiration turned to pity. The weather had become extremely cold, and the reporter was too poor to buy the necessary clothing to protect himself from the elements. It was obvious that the young man's devotion to duty was causing him great personal discomfort.

One night the affair came to an interesting climax. McKinley was riding in a closed carriage, while the critical reporter sat shivering on the driver's seat outside. McKinley stood the man's chattering teeth as long as he could, then he stopped the carriage and said, "Young man, come here. Put on this overcoat, and ride inside with me."

"But, Mr. McKinley," the young man stammered, "don't you know who I am? I've been ripping you to pieces during this campaign, and I don't intend to stop."

"Yes, yes, I know who you are," replied McKinley, "but for now just put on this coat and get inside where it is warm."

A petty person, an arrogant person, would have said, "You fool, stay out there and freeze. It would serve you right for your unfair criticism of me." But McKinley was neither petty nor arrogant.

In the following days of the campaign the reporter still opposed McKinley's campaign, because it was his paper's policy, but he never again wrote anything unfair or biased about the future president.

My true religion is kindness.

THE 14TH DALAI LAMA OF TIBET

The older you get, the more you realize that kindness is synonymous with happiness.

LIONEL BARRYMORE (1878-1954)
Actor

Kind words can be short and easy to speak, but their echoes are truly endless.

MOTHER TERESA
Catholic missionary

THE STORY IS TOLD that Samuel Hanagid, an 11th century Spanish-Jewish poet who was prime minister to the king of Granada, was once insulted by an enemy in the presence of the king.

The king was so angered that he ordered his prime minister to punish the offender by cutting out his tongue. Contrary to the king's mandate, Samuel treated his enemy with utmost kindness. When the king learned that his order had not been carried out, he was greatly astonished.

Samuel was ready with a pleasant answer. He said, "I have carried out your order, Your Majesty, I have cut out his evil tongue and have given him instead a kindly tongue."

Often we are caught in the snare of the old adage that we must fight fire with fire. We retaliate against hate with hate, and we answer anger with anger. All we really succeed in doing is magnifying the problem, for by increasing a fire all we simply do is intensify the heat.

The true way to extinguish a fire is with cool water. Likewise, the effective way to quench a quarrel is with cooling and soothing words. Most arguments are rooted in irrational hate; before reason can be applied to relationships, hate must be dispelled. This can only be done when the voice is soft, the temper is low, and the regard for others is gentle. The real antidote to anger is, obviously, pleasantness.

RABBI BERNARD S. RASKAS
Heart of Wisdom
United Synagogue of America

Kind hearts are the garden,

Kind thoughts are the roots,

Kind words are the blossoms,

Kind deeds are the fruits.

JOHN RUSKIN (1819-1900)
English writer

DURING THE DEVASTATING earthquakes in Kobe, Japan, an American newscaster did a short piece on a Japanese woman who set up a makeshift store out of boxes, selling flashlights and batteries.

When the commentator asked why she wasn't selling them for more than the regular price, the woman answered, "Why would I want to profit from someone else's suffering?"

KNOWLEDGE ❖ ❖ ❖

Arthur Motley, former U.S. Chamber of Commerce president, observed: "Few executives are smart enough to remember all they know."

The only things worth learning are the things you learn after you know it all.

HARRY S. TRUMAN (1884-1972)
33rd President of the U.S.

Knowledge is free at the library. Just bring your own container.

Between the semi-educated, who offer simplistic answers to complex questions, and the overeducated, who offer complicated answers to simple questions, it is a wonder that any questions get satisfactorily settled at all.

SYDNEY J. HARRIS (1917-1986)
Syndicated columnist

All too often, people are afraid to admit they don't have all the answers, so they just make them up. They elaborate on what they don't understand to the point of embarrassment. Instead, all they had to do was say, "I don't know, but I'll find out." Remember, nobody can fault you for admitting you don't know everything. In fact, they might even admire you.

BILL DANIELS
Cable TV executive

The world does not require so much to be informed as to be reminded.

HANNAH MORE

IT IS SAID that scientific knowledge is growing at an exponential rate. To appreciate what that means, consider the story of a farmer who brought his horse to be shod and asked what it would cost. The blacksmith said he would charge a penny for the first nail, 2 cents for the second, 4 cents for the third, and so on. The farmer, innocent of mathematics, agreed. For eight nails in each shoe, or 32 nails altogether, his bill came to $42,949,642.95

An exponential rate of growth is an awesome thing.

LAUGHTER ❖ ❖ ❖

Seven days without laughter makes one weak.

JOEL GOODMAN
Humor educator

You grow up the day you have your first real laugh—at yourself.

ETHEL BARRYMORE (1879-1959)
Actress

Laughter is the best revenge.

He who laughs, lasts.

MARY PETTIBONE POOLE

Laughter is a tranquilizer with no side effects.

Those who can't laugh at themselves leave the job to others.

When people are laughing, they're generally not killing each other.

ALAN ALDA
Actor

❖ ❖ ❖ **LAZINESS**

Laziness is nothing more than the habit of resting before you get tired.

JULES RENARD (1864-1910)
French writer

It is impossible to enjoy idling thoroughly unless one has plenty of work to do.

JEROME K. JEROME (1859-1927)
English writer

ABRAHAM LINCOLN ONCE TOOK a sack of grain to a mill whose proprietor was known to be the laziest man in Illinois. After watching the miller for a while, the future president commented wearily, "I can eat that grain as fast as you're grinding it."

"Indeed," grunted the miller, "and how long do you think you could keep that up?"

"Until I starved to death," replied Lincoln.

LEADERSHIP ❖ ❖ ❖

One of the tests of leadership is the ability to recognize a problem before it becomes an emergency.

ARNOLD GLASGOW

Policies are many,
Principles are few,
Policies will change,
Principles never do.

JOHN C. MAXWELL
Developing the Leader Within You
Thomas Nelson Publishers

What I wanted to be when I grew up was—in charge.

BRIGADIER GENERAL WILMA VAUGHT
U.S. Air Force

A COMPANY PRESIDENT wanted to soften the news that he had already made a decision on a half-million dollar capital investment.

Meeting with middle management, he said, "Those in favor of spending $500,000, raise your hands." All raised their hands.

"Opposed, raise your hands." He alone raised his hand.

"Boy," he smiled, "that was close. You folks almost outvoted me."

ESTHER BLUMENFELD and LYNNE ALPERN
Humor at Work
Peachtree Publishers

A leader's job is to make it easy to do the right thing and difficult to do the wrong thing.

GOOD LEADERSHIP is an elusive mix of traits. It combines a firm grasp of the technical details with a handle on the more intuitive, human skills of getting along with others and expanding their horizons. Good leaders know how to inspire others by encouraging them to break past their self-imposed limits and release those fears that halt success.

DONNA RAE SMITH
The Power of Building Your Bright Side
Wynwood Publishing

There are two ways of exerting one's strength: pushing down or pulling up.

BOOKER T. WASHINGTON (1856-1915)
Educator and writer

MANAGEMENT is bottom-line focus: How can I best accomplish certain things? Leadership deals with the top line: What are the things I want to accomplish?

Management is efficiency in climbing the ladder of success; leadership determines whether the ladder is leaning against the right wall.

STEPHEN R. COVEY
Writer

Leadership is a verb, not a noun.

BILL GORE (1912-1986)
Founder, W.L. Gore & Associates

131

DELEGATION: *A Parable*

ONCE UPON A TIME there was a Little Red Hen who owned a wheat field. "Who will help me harvest the wheat?" she asked.

"Not I," said the pig. "I don't know how."

"Not I," said the cow. "I'm too clumsy."

"Not I," said the dog. "I'm busy with some other things."

So the Little Red Hen did it herself.

"Who will help me grind the wheat into flour?" she asked.

"Not I," said the pig. "That's another vocation in which I'm untrained."

"Not I," said the cow. "You could do it much more efficiently."

"Not I," said the dog. "I'd love to, but I'm involved in some matters of greater urgency. Some other time, perhaps."

So she did it herself.

"Who will help me make some bread?" asked the Little Red Hen.

"Not I," said the pig. "Nobody ever taught me how."

"Not I," said the cow. "You're more experienced and could do it in half the time."

"Not I," said the dog. "I've made some other plans for the afternoon. But I'll help you next time."

So she did it herself.

That evening, when guests arrived for her big dinner party, the Little Red Hen had nothing to serve them except bread. She had been so busy doing work that could have been done by others that she had forgotten to plan a main course, prepare a dessert, or even get out the silverware. The evening was a disaster, and she lived unhappily ever after.

MORAL: A good leader will find a way to involve others to the extent of their ability. To do the job yourself is the chicken way out.

EDWIN C. BLISS
Getting Things Done
Bantam Books

The person who is worthy of being a leader will never complain of the stupidity of his helpers, of the ingratitude of mankind, or of the inappreciation of the public. These things are all a part of the great game of life, and to meet them and not go down before them in discouragement and defeat is the final proof of power.

ELBERT HUBBARD (1856-1915)
Writer

———————

The speed of the pack is determined by the speed of the leader.

———————

What a man dislikes in his superiors, let him not display in the treatment of his inferiors.

TSANG SIN
Disciple of Confucius

———————

IN FOUR YEARS of executive seminars conducted by Santa Clara University and the Tom Peters Group/Learning Systems, more than 5,200 senior managers were asked to describe the characteristics they most admire in a leader. Here are the top 10 characteristics, as reported in *Management Review* magazine:

1. Honest
2 Competent
3. Forward-looking
4. Inspiring
5. Intelligent

6. Fair-minded
7. Broad-minded
8. Courageous
9. Straightforward
10. Imaginative

Secrets of Executive Success
Rodale Press

———————

133

Leaders create energy in others by instilling purpose.

Obviously, people must have knowledge in their fields. But the greatest success and financial reward will go to people who have more: the ability to express their ideas, to assume leadership, to arouse enthusiasm and cooperation—in short, the ability to bring out the best in others.

Leaders have two important characteristics: First, they're going somewhere; second, they're able to persuade other people to go along with them.

Authority is a poor substitute for leadership.

JOHN L. BECKLEY
Founder, The Economics Press, Inc.

If you treat a man as he is, he will remain as he is; if you treat him as he ought to be and could be, he will become as he ought to be and could be.

JOHANN WOLFGANG VON GOETHE (1749-1832)
German writer

DONALD SMITH was an agent for the Hudson Bay Company in Canada's wilderness many years ago. Word came to his post that a trapper had some valuable furs, which he would not sell to the company because of complaints over previous trades.

Young Smith set out to see him, tramping 20 miles across the snow to the trapper's cabin. He arrived just at sunset. His reception was as chilly as the weather. Nevertheless, Smith asked to spend the night, since it was five more miles to the next cabin.

Frontier hospitality demanded that his request be granted. That was the way Smith had planned it. In his coat pocket there were a few pieces of candy and some colored pictures for the children. Smith addressed the trapper's wife as "Madam" and helped her with the fire and the meal. Not a word was said about furs.

The next morning, as Smith was leaving, the sulky trapper exclaimed, "Aren't you going to look at my furs?" He then rushed out some of the valuable furs, set his own price, and Smith gladly paid.

Donald Smith knew the value of waiting for the other person to make the first move—to, in effect, give his consent to be led. He was later to go on to build the Canadian Pacific railway and become head of the Hudson Bay Company, one of the most venerable (its charter of incorporation was dated May 2, 1670) companies in the world.

Patience to wait for the other person to make the first move always helps a leader. That first move shows a willingness to follow or to do business. It is basic to good leadership.

———————

WE ARE ALL ATTRACTED to books and articles that promise the "rules" of successful leadership. Leadership is still an art and not a science. And just like in any art, there are no definitive "rules."

The English novelist W. Somerset Maugham said, "There are three rules for writing a novel. Unfortunately, no one knows what they are."

It's the same with leadership. There probably are three rules for successful leadership. Unfortunately, no one knows what they are either.

———————

LEARNING ❖ ❖ ❖

EVERYTHING YOU HAVE TO KNOW
ABOUT LEARNING IN A NUTSHELL

No matter what you want to learn, there are four stages:

1. **Unconscious Incompetent.** You don't know that you don't know.

2. **Conscious Incompetent.** You know that you don't know.

3. **Conscious Competent.** You know that you know.

4. **Unconscious Competent.** You know it without thinking.

LIFE IS A LEARNING PROCESS, as this beautiful bit of free verse by Veronica A. Shoffstall tells us:

After a while you learn the subtle difference
Between holding a hand and chaining a soul,
And you learn that love doesn't mean leaning
And company doesn't mean security.
And you begin to learn that kisses aren't contracts
And presents aren't promises,
And you begin to accept your defeats
With your head up and your eyes open
With the grace of a woman, not the grief of a child,
And you learn to build all your roads on today
Because tomorrow's ground is too uncertain for plans
And futures have a way of falling down in mid-flight.
After a while you learn
That even sunshine burns if you get too much.
So you plant your garden and decorate your own soul,
Instead of waiting for someone to bring you flowers.
And you learn that you really can endure . . .

That you really are strong
And you really do have worth . . .
And you learn . . .
With every good-bye, you learn.

◆   ◆   ◆   **LIBRARY**

The library is not a shrine for the worship of books. It is not a temple where literary incense must be burned or where one's devotion to the bound book is expressed in ritual. A library, to modify the famous metaphor of Socrates, should be the delivery room for the birth of ideas—a place where history comes to life.

NORMAN COUSINS (1915-1990)
Writer and editor

I am the library.
I am neither walls nor shelves.
Nor even the books that stand in rows.
I am the wisdom of the universe
Captured and arranged for you.
I am an open door.
ENTER . . . .

Never lend books, for no one ever returns them. The only books I have in my library are books that other folks lent me.

ANATOLE FRANCE (1844-1924)
French novelist

Books are the quietest and most patient of teachers.

LIFE ❖ ❖ ❖

Half of life is *if*.

I would rather think of life as a good book. The further you get into it, the more it begins to come together and make sense.

RABBI HAROLD KUSHNER
When All You've Ever Wanted Isn't Enough
Summit Books

Life is like a grindstone—whether it grinds you down or polishes you up depends on what you're made of.

Life is made up of two phases: In the first you try to make a name for yourself and in the second you try to keep it.

I've always told my children that life is like a layer cake. You get to put one layer on top of the other and whether you frost it or not is up to you.

ANN RICHARDS
Former governor of Texas

Since life is short, we need to make it broad. Since life is brief, we need to make it bright.

ELLA WHEELER WILCOX (1850-1919)
Poet

To the question of your life, you are the only answer.

To the problems of your life, you are the only solution.

JO COUDERT
American television executive

Life is 10 percent what you make it and 90 percent how you take it.

WHEN THE LATE NADINE STAIR of Louisville, Kentucky, was 85 years old, she was asked what she would do if she had her life to live over again.

"I'd make more mistakes next time," she said. "I'd relax. I would limber up. I would be sillier than I have been this trip. I would take fewer things seriously. I would take more chances. I would climb more mountains and swim more rivers. I would eat more ice cream and less beans. I would perhaps have more actual troubles, but I'd have fewer imaginary ones.

"You see, I'm one of those people who live sensibly and sanely hour after hour, day after day. Oh, I've had my moments, and if I had to do it over again, I'd have more of them. In fact, I'd try to have nothing else. Just moments, one after another, instead of living so many years ahead of each day. I've been one of those persons who never goes anywhere without a thermometer, a hot water bottle, and a raincoat. If I had to do it over again, I would travel lighter than I have.

"If I had my life to live over, I would start barefoot earlier in the spring and stay that way later in the fall. I would go to more dances. I would ride more merry-go-rounds, I would pick more daisies."

Life is what happens to you while you're making other plans.

Every important life story has two aspects: the things a man has energy enough to do, and the things a man has stability enough to stand.

HARRY EMERSON FOSDICK (1878-1969)
Religious leader

A most pleasant good wish was uttered by a fellow named Kemmons Wilson. "As you slide down the banister of life," he said, "may all the splinters be pointed in the right direction."

MOST OF US miss out on life's big prizes. The Pulitzer. The Nobel. Oscars. Tonys. Emmys. But we're all eligible for life's small pleasures. A pat on the back. A kiss behind the ear. A four-pound bass. A full moon. An empty parking space. A crackling fire. A great meal. A glorious sunset. Hot soup. Cold beer. Don't fret about copping life's grand rewards. Enjoy its tiny delights. There are plenty for all of us.

From an advertisement for
United Technologies Corporation

You must learn day by day, year by year, to broaden your horizon. The more you love, the more you are interested in, the more you enjoy, the more you are indignant about—the more you have left when anything happens.

ETHEL BARRYMORE (1879-1959)
Actress

It is something to be able to paint a particular picture, or to carve a statue, and so to make a few objects beautiful; but it is far more glorious to carve and paint the very atmosphere and

medium through which we look . . . . To affect the quality of the day—that is the highest of arts.

HENRY DAVID THOREAU (1817-1862)
Writer

How wonderful it is that nobody need wait a single moment before starting to improve the world.

ANNE FRANK (1929-1945)
Holocaust diarist

Our conduct is influenced not by our experience, but by expectations.

GEORGE BERNARD SHAW
Iris

I think the purpose of life is to be happy, to be   .l, to be responsible, to be honorable, to be compassionate. i   ,, above all, to matter, to count, to stand for something, to have made some difference that you lived at all.

LEO ROSTEN (1908-1997)
Writer

The most beautiful experience we can have is the mysterious. It is the fundamental emotion which stands at the cradle of true art and true science.

ALBERT EINSTEIN (1879-1955)
Physicist

The be-all and end-all of life should not be to get rich, but to enrich the world.

B.C. FORBES (1880-1954)
Magazine publisher

Our lives begin to end the minute we become silent about things that matter.

MARTIN LUTHER KING, JR. (1929-1968)
Civil rights leader

Experience is the hardest kind of teacher. It gives you the test first and the lesson afterward.

"LIFE IS A GAMBLE," a Mother Cabbage told her offspring, Brussels Sprout. "You have to weather storms and drought. You have to fend off animals, bugs, mold, and rot. But if you hang in there, you'll grow."

"I'll try," said the little Sprout. "But how long does this take? When should I stop growing?"

"As with any other gamble," said Mother Cabbage. "Quit when you're a head."

LISTENING ❖ ❖ ❖

Talk to people about themselves, and they'll listen for hours.

BENJAMIN DISRAELI (1804-1881)
British prime minister

There is no greater loan than a sympathetic ear.

FRANK TYGER

The six steps to becoming a better listener form a LADDER:

L: Look at the person speaking to you.

A: Ask questions.

D: Don't interrupt.

D: Don't change the subject.

E: Empathize.

R: Respond verbally and nonverbally.

It seems rather incongruous that in a society of super-sophisticated communication, we often suffer from a shortage of listeners.

ERMA BOMBECK (1927-1996)
Syndicated columnist

A good listener is a silent flatterer.

Good listeners are not only popular everywhere, but after a while they know something.

A high school class in music appreciation was asked the difference between listening and hearing. At first there was no response. Finally, a hand went up and a youngster offered this wise definition: "Listening is wanting to hear."

WE LISTEN TOO MUCH to the telephone, and we listen too little to nature. The wind is one of my sounds—a lonely sound, perhaps,

143

but soothing. Everybody should have their personal sounds to listen for—sounds that make them exhilarated and alive, or quiet and calm. As a matter of fact, one of the greatest sounds of all—and to me it is a sound—is utter, complete silence.

ANDRE KOSTELANETZ (1901-1980)
Conductor

A wise old owl sat on an oak,
The more he saw the less he spoke;
The less he spoke the more he heard;
Why aren't we like that wise old bird?

EDWARD H. RICHARDS
Poet

The funny thing about human beings is that we tend to respect the intelligence of, and eventually to like, those who listen attentively to our ideas even if they continue to disagree with us.

S.I. HAYAKAWA (1906-1992)
Educator and politician

I make progress by having people around me who are smarter than I am—and listening to them. And I assume that everyone is smarter about something than I am.

HENRY KAISER (1882-1967)
Industrialist

A certain supervisor had trouble communicating with his workers. Finally, in desperation, the supervisor pleaded: "Don't listen to what I say. Listen to what I mean!"

WHEN A MAN whose marriage was in trouble sought his advice, the Master said, "You must learn to listen to your wife."

The man took this advice to heart and returned after a month to say he had learned to listen to every word his wife was saying.

Said the Master with a smile, "Now go home and listen to every word she isn't saying."

> ANTHONY DE MELLO, S.J.
> *One Minute Wisdom*
> Doubleday

We're born with two ears and one mouth. That ought to tell us something.

❖ ❖ ❖ LONGEVITY

ALBERT AMATEAU, 105 years old, says he expected longevity. "I lived my life in such a way that I knew I would live beyond 100," he explains.

Being an avid walker has always been part of his life. He was once examined by an incredulous physician, 50 years his junior, who was amazed to hear that Mr. Amateau walked four or five miles every day.

"What do you do when it rains?" asked the doctor.

"I put on a raincoat," the old man replied.

> SALLI RASBERRY and PADI SELWYN
> *Living Your Life Out Loud*
> Pocket Books

145

If you ask me the secret to longevity, I would tell you that you have to work at taking care of your health. But a lot of it is attitude. I'm alive out of sheer determination, honey!

SARAH L. DELANY and A. ELIZABETH DELANY
with AMY HILL HEARTH
Having Our Say: The Delany Sisters' First 100 Years
Kodansha International

Methuselah ate what he found on his plate,
And never, as people do now,
Did he note the amount of the calorie count;
He ate it because it was chow.

He wasn't disturbed as at a dinner he sat,
Devouring a roast or a pie,
To think it was lacking in the right kind of fat
Or a couple of vitamins shy.

He cheerfully chewed each species of food,
Unmindful of troubles or fears
Lest his health might be hurt by some fancy dessert;
And he lived over 900 years!

A light heart lives long.

WILLIAM SHAKESPEARE (1564-1616)
English writer

A PIOUS MAN who had reached the age of 105 suddenly stopped going to synagogue. Alarmed by the old fellow's absence after so many years of faithful attendance, the rabbi went to see him.

He found him in good health, so the rabbi asked, "How come after all these years we don't see you at services?"

The old man looked around and lowered his voice. "I'll tell you, Rabbi," he whispered. "When I got to be 90, I thought, any day God will take me. But then I got to be 95, then 100, then 105. So I figured that God is a busy man and He must have forgotten about me . . . and I don't want to remind Him."

JAMES DENT (1928-1992)
Charleston Gazette

———————

WILLARD SCOTT, of *Today* show fame, makes it a practice to visit the elderly, particularly centenarians, wherever he travels. In talking to them, he's found one common thread: Every centenarian, and everyone with a shot at reaching that milestone, is blessed with an easygoing nature.

Without exception, these people are calm and levelheaded, and they take life as it comes. In life, they've learned to accept the cards they have been dealt.

Whether they were born that way or became that way over the years is not important. What is important is that they are that way now, and we can all learn from that.

———————

In spite of illness, in spite of the archenemy sorrow, one can remain alive long past the usual date of disintegration if one is unafraid of change, insatiable in intellectual curiosity, interested in big things, and happy in small ways.

EDITH WHARTON (1862-1937)
Novelist

———————

147

LOVE ❖ ❖ ❖

Only in opera do people die of love.

FREDA BRIGHT

Love is like quicksilver in the hand. Leave the fingers open and it stays. Clutch it, and it darts away.

DOROTHY PARKER (1893-1967)
Writer

Love lives in cottages as well as in castles.

Love calls for open arms. With arms open you allow love to come and go as it wills, freely, for it will do so anyway. If you close your arms about love, you'll find you are left only holding yourself.

LEO BUSCAGLIA
Educator and writer

Love may not make the world go around, but it sure makes the trip worthwhile.

How do you know that love is gone? If you said that you would be there at seven and you get there by nine, and he or she has not called the police yet—it's gone.

MARLENE DIETRICH (1901-1992)
German actress

We too often love things and use people, when we should be using things and loving people.

Love looks through a telescope; envy through a microscope.

JOSH BILLINGS (1818-1885)
Humorist

Love yourself first and everything else falls into line. You really have to love yourself to get anything done in this world.

LUCILLE BALL (1911-1989)
Actress

If we suddenly discovered that we had only five minutes left to say all we wanted to say, every telephone booth would be occupied by people trying to call up other people to tell them that they loved them.

CHRISTOPHER MORLEY (1890-1957)
Writer

Love is a fruit in season at all times, and within reach of every hand.

MOTHER TERESA
Catholic missionary

In love you must give three times before you take once.

BRAZILIAN PROVERB

149

WHAT IS TRUE LOVE? The late Father James Keller, founder of The Christophers, put it this way:

Love delights in giving attention rather than attracting it.
Love finds the element of good and builds on it.
Love does not magnify defects.
Love is a flame that warms but never burns.
Love knows how to disagree without becoming disagreeable.
Love rejoices at the success of others instead of being envious.

Love is an irresistible desire to be irresistibly desired.

ROBERT FROST (1874-1963)
Poet

Love is an unusual game. There are either two winners or none.

If I could reinvent the alphabet, I would put *U* and *I* together.

Love is what makes two people sit in the middle of a bench when there's plenty of room at both ends.

The most important thing a father can do for his children is to love their mother.

THE GERMAN PHILOSOPHER and scholar Moses Mendelssohn (1729-1786) was born a hunchback. Despite this deformity, which could have soured him on life forever, Mendelssohn achieved a maturity and wisdom few people ever do.

While on a trip to Hamburg as a young man, Mendelssohn met a rich merchant who had a beautiful young daughter, Frumtje. The young man fell hopelessly in love with her. She, too, was mature beyond her years, and despite his obvious physical defect, she was attracted to his gentleness, his charm, and his brilliant mind.

Mendelssohn stayed several weeks in Hamburg, spending much of his time with this lovely young woman he had fallen in love with at first sight. When it finally came time to leave, he worked up enough nerve to speak to her father. It was either that or lose her forever.

The rich and powerful merchant hesitated for a long time. Mendelssohn finally asked him to speak his thoughts frankly.

"Well," said the older man, "you are known throughout Germany as a most brilliant young man. And yet . . . I must tell you my child was a bit frightened when she first saw you."

"Because I am a hunchback?"

Sadly, the merchant nodded.

Downcast, but not defeated, Mendelssohn asked only one last favor—the privilege of seeing her once more before he left. Admitted to her room, he found her busy with needlework. He spoke at first of various matters, then carefully and gradually, he led the conversation to the subject that was nearest to his heart. "Do you believe," he asked, "that marriages are made in heaven?"

"Yes," she said, "for that is our faith."

"And it is true," he said gently. "Now let me tell you about something strange that happened when I was born. As you know, at a child's birth, according to our tradition, they call out in heaven that the birth has occurred. And when it is a boy, they announce, 'Such-and-such boy will have this-or-that girl for a wife.'

"Well, there I was, just born, and I heard the name of my

future wife announced. At the same time, I heard the great far-off voice say, 'Unfortunately, the poor little girl, Frumtje, will have a terrible hump on her back.' Quick as a flash, I cried out, 'O Lord God, if a girl is hunchbacked, she will grow up bitter and hard. Please give her hump to me and let her develop into a well-formed, lovely, and charming young lady.' "

Mendelssohn waited for her reaction. Slowly, Frumtje looked up. She dropped her needlework, rose, and approached him with arms outstretched.

The merchant gave his consent and they were soon married, living a long and fruitful life together.

A YOUNG WOMAN was explaining to a friend why she had decided to marry one man rather than another. "When I was with John," she said, "I felt he was the cleverest person in the world."

"Then why didn't you choose him?" the puzzled friend asked.

"Because when I'm with Bill I feel *I'm* the cleverest person in the world."

Being unwanted, unloved, uncared for, forgotten by everybody, I think that is a much greater hunger, a much greater poverty than the person who has nothing to eat. We must find each other.

MOTHER TERESA
Catholic missionary

WE'VE SAID this before in other ways: If you love someone, tell them. Now. Even if you just "care" for them. Don't put it off. Tell them now.

It's a message worth repeating and it was brought home to us once again when we read Leo Buscaglia's book *Living,*

Loving & Learning (Fawcett Columbine).

In it, the writer, counselor, and University of Southern California professor used a poem called "Things You Didn't Do" to emphasize what can happen if you put things off. The person who sent it to Professor Buscaglia asked to remain anonymous, but some composer ought to track her down and ask permission to put music to these words:

> *Remember the day I borrowed your*
> *brand new car and I dented it?*
> *I thought you'd kill me, but you didn't.*
>
> *And remember the time I dragged you*
> *to the beach, and you said it would*
> *rain, and it did?*
> *I thought you'd say, "I told you so."*
> *But you didn't.*
>
> *Do you remember the time I flirted with*
> *all the guys to make you jealous, and*
> *you were?*
> *I thought you'd leave me, but you didn't.*
>
> *Do you remember the time I spilled*
> *strawberry pie all over your car rug?*
> *I thought you'd hit me, but you didn't.*
>
> *And remember the time I forgot to tell*
> *you the dance was formal and you*
> *showed up in jeans?*
> *I thought you'd drop me, but you didn't.*
>
> *Yes, there were lots of things you didn't do.*
> *But you put up with me, and you loved*
> *me, and you protected me.*
> *There were lots of things I wanted to*
> *make up to you when you returned*
> *from Vietnam,*
> *But you didn't.*

LUCK ⬧ ⬧ ⬧

I don't know anything about luck. I've never banked on it, and I'm afraid of people who do. Luck to me is something else; hard work—and realizing what is opportunity and what isn't.

LUCILLE BALL (1911-1989)
Actress

Luck = Good Planning + Careful Execution

MAX GUNTHER wrote a book called *The Luck Factor*, in which he speculated on why some people are luckier than others. He discovered that those who were lucky more often tried things more frequently than those who did not, thus increasing their success. He theorized that the more times you cast your net in the water, the better your chance of catching a fish.

MANAGEMENT ⬧ ⬧ ⬧

KENNETH BLANCHARD, the business-motivational writer, says talking to trainers of killer whales at Sea World aquarium in San Diego, California, taught him something about managing employees.

Many managers still think that fear and money are the best motivators. Chuck Tompkins, supervisor of animal behavior at Sea World, doesn't agree. In his case, he says the relationship the animals have with their trainers is far more important than fear or food, which is the animal equivalent of money.

At Sea World, the animals don't fear the trainer, because the trainers make no attempt to frighten or dominate them. Instead, the trainers get to know the animals, just as good managers take a personal interest in the well-being of their employees.

Occasionally, the whales do misbehave and the trainers have to take action. The trainers know that their responses to such behavior must be predictable, so they have standardized their approach to dealing with it.

The trainers use what they call the three-second stare. When the whales float on their backs, for instance, instead of leaping from the water, the trainer stares at them for three seconds. The whales get bored with that response quickly and try something else.

But when the whales perform properly, the trainers do any one of many unpredictable things. They pat them on the head, feed them fish, or scratch their tongue (a killer whale's favorite treat). The whales learn that performing the tricks is better than not performing.

Managers can draw from this the lesson that a positive relationship with workers is a powerful motivator. To gain the respect and loyalty of employees, a manager should emphasize the positive aspects of each employee and de-emphasize the negative. Catch people doing right and let them know that you have.

COMPANIES THAT ATTRACT a high proportion of peak performers are run by managers willing to give power to gain power, not by people who collect power to squelch others.

David Ogilvy, founder of the advertising giant Ogilvy and Mather, reinforced the importance of that principle among his executives by sending a Russian doll to each person newly appointed to head an office in the Ogilvy and Mather chain.

The doll contains five progressively smaller dolls. The message inside the smallest one reads: "If each of us hires people who are smaller than we are, we shall become a company of dwarfs.

But if each of us hires people who are bigger than we are, Ogilvy and Mather will become a company of giants."

Before Ogilvy retired, the company succeeded in doing just that.

———————————

Good human relationships are just good business, but it starts at the top. Give me a man who has an understanding of human nature and an understanding of workers' problems and the fundamental knowledge of the management components and you have an unbeatable combination. Good human relationships are not worth anything unless there is sincerity, fairness, and impartiality. It doesn't come from books. It comes from the heart.

WILLIAM A. PATTERSON

———————————

THE FOUR-TO-ONE RULE

For every criticism you make of a worker's performance, give him or her four compliments.

Fortune Cookies
Vintage Books

———————————

I believe managing is like holding a dove in your hand. If you hold it too tightly, you kill it, but if you hold it too loosely, you lose it.

TOMMY LASORDA
Baseball manager

———————————

❖ ❖ ❖ MARRIAGE

LOTS OF PEOPLE have asked me what Gracie and I did to make our marriage work. It's simple—we didn't do anything.

I think the trouble with a lot of people is that they work too hard at staying married. They make a business out of it.

When you work too hard at a business, you get tired; and when you get tired, you get grouchy; and when you get grouchy, you start fighting; and when you start fighting you're out of business.

GEORGE BURNS
Living It Up
Putnam

❖ ❖ ❖ MATURITY

MATURITY IS:

the ability to stick with a job until it's finished;

the ability to do a job without being supervised;

the ability to carry money without spending it; and

the ability to bear an injustice without wanting to get even.

ABIGAIL VAN BUREN
Syndicated columnist

I have lived in this world just long enough to look carefully the second time into things that I am most certain of the first time.

JOSH BILLINGS (1818-1885)
Humorist

157

We are only young once, but we can be immature indefinitely.

❖ ❖ ❖ MEETINGS

TIRED OF TOO many meetings? In his wonderful little book *How to Run a Successful Meeting in Half the Time* (Simon & Schuster), Milo O. Frank offers this tongue-in-cheek solution:

"In the 17th century, an edict was passed by Lord Protector of England, Oliver Cromwell, that in order to curtail the savage practices of some of his troops (ranging from rape to pillage and murder), a new procedure would be initiated. The offending soldier and his entire company would assemble underneath the local gallows and hold a meeting.

"This meeting, in main, would consist of the rolling of dice. Everyone would participate. The man who lost would be hanged. Not necessarily the instigator of the crime, but simply the man who lost.

"The results were fewer crimes, fewer troops—and fewer meetings."

IN THE CONFERENCE ROOM of a large corporation was a framed motto expressing the sentiments of the president. It's no longer there, but its message was: *Intelligence is no substitute for information; enthusiasm is no substitute for capacity; willingness is no substitute for experience.* The motto is gone because one morning, after a series of meetings, someone had added: *A meeting is no substitute for progress.*

❖ ❖ ❖ MISSION

**Here is a test to find whether your mission on earth is finished:
If you're alive, it isn't.**

> RICHARD BACH
> *Illusions*
> Delacorte Press

Make your life a mission—not an intermission.

> ARNOLD GLASGOW

❖ ❖ ❖ MISTAKES

Do not fear mistakes. There are none.

> MILES DAVIS (1926-1991)
> Jazz musician

NO MATTER HOW MUCH effort you put into something, no matter how well you prepare, you will make mistakes. Fallibility is human. It's how we learn. Nobody learns to walk without falling, to ski without a few headplants, to surf without wiping out. No writer, salesperson, senator, or suitor escapes rejection.

Who learns a language faster, a person who studies endlessly before attempting a conversation or a person who jumps right in undaunted by making a lot of errors? Says former IBM Chairman Tom Watson, "If you want to succeed, double your failure rate."

> ROBERT KRIEGEL and DAVID BRANDT
> *Sacred Cows Make the Best Burgers*
> Warner Books

159

BRUCE BARTON, one of the original partners in the legendary advertising agency of Batten, Barton, Durstine & Osborne, once told the following story:

"One day on my first job as a young man in New York, a matter came up about which I happened to have the facts. My boss disagreed, and though I put up a good argument, he somewhat abruptly overruled me.

"I was living those days in a room in the 23rd Street YMCA in New York for which I paid seven dollars a week. His home was a fair-sized mansion requiring 10 servants. The morning after our argument, the telephone rang while I was dressing, and I wondered who in New York could be after me so early.

"To my amazement it was the boss. Said he: 'I have been thinking about our discussion of yesterday, and I just want you to know you were right and I was wrong.'

"The boss with an income of $100,000 a year, calling on a $40-a-week youngster to say, 'I was wrong!' He had been 100 percent with me; after that he was the biggest man in town.

"Years have gone by and I have known all sorts and conditions of men and women in business, in the professions, and in politics. As an employer, it has interested me to observe how they divide into two classes: those who feel they have lowered themselves by admitting a mistake, and so try in every way to rationalize it, and those who come out in forthright fashion and admit the facts."

———

IN HIS AUTOBIOGRAPHY *The Tumult and the Shouting*, the great sports columnist Grantland Rice once gave this advice about past mistakes:

"Because golf exposes the flaws of the human swing—a basically simple maneuver—it causes more self-torture than any game short of Russian roulette. The quicker the average golfer can forget the shot he has dubbed or knocked off line—and con-

160

centrate on the next shot—the sooner he begins to improve and enjoy golf. Like life, golf can be humbling. However, little good comes from brooding about mistakes we've made. The next shot, in golf or life, is the big one.

"Walter Hagen, a dazzling ornament to the history of sport, had the soundest golf philosophy I've ever known. More important, he applied it.

" 'Grant,' he said, 'I expect to make at least seven mistakes each round. Therefore, when I make a bad shot I don't worry about it. It's just one of those seven.'

"I saw Hagen make 19 mistakes during one round in a North and South Open at Pinehurst in 1924. He finished with a 71, ultimately winning the tournament. A mistake meant nothing to him."

The greatest blunders, like the thickest ropes, are often compounded of a multitude of strands. Take the rope apart, separate it into the small threads that compose it, and you can break them one by one. You think, "That is all there was!" But twist them all together and you have something tremendous.

VICTOR HUGO
Les Miserables

ONE OF THE TRAITS that made Abraham Lincoln a great leader was his ability to keep an open mind. This required a basic humility and a willingness to admit his mistakes. Many people react with stubbornness and anger when their mistakes are pointed out.

During the American Civil War, Lincoln, under severe political pressure, signed an order to transfer regiments from one field of battle to another. But Edwin M. Stanton, Lincoln's Secretary of War, refused to carry out the orders.

"Lincoln is a damn fool for ever signing the order," Stanton snorted.

The remark was passed on to Lincoln, who did not disagree. "If Stanton said I'm a damn fool, then I must be one," the President replied. "He is nearly always right in military matters. I'll step over and find out what his reasoning is."

Stanton, much more knowledgeable in the science of warfare than Lincoln, convinced his commander-in-chief of the folly of the order. Lincoln promptly rescinded it, saving the Union troops from a disaster that otherwise would have cost thousands of lives.

A smart manager makes a mistake worthwhile by being big enough to admit it, strong enough to correct it, and intelligent enough to profit from the process.

MONEY ❖ ❖ ❖

Money is a wonderful thing, but it is possible to pay too high a price for it.

ALEXANDER BLOCH
Conductor

The easiest way to teach children the value of money is to borrow from them.

COMIC ACTOR STEVE MARTIN claims he has a plan that everyone can use to avoid paying taxes on a million dollars.

Someone asked him to go through the plan, step by step. "First," Martin said, "get a million dollars. That first step is the hardest one."

162

Money may be the husk of many things, but not the kernel. It brings you food, but not appetite; medicine, but not health; acquaintances, but not friends; servants, but not faithfulness; days of joy, but not peace and happiness.

HENRIK IBSEN (1828-1906)
Norwegian writer

There is nothing wrong with men possessing riches. The wrong comes when riches possess men.

BILLY GRAHAM
Religious leader

A YOUNG MAN once asked God how long a million years was to Him.

God replied, "A million years to me is just like a single second in your time."

Then the young man asked God what a million dollars was to Him.

God replied, "A million dollars to me is just like a single penny to you."

Then the young man got his courage up and asked: "God, could I have one of your pennies?"

God smiled and replied, "Certainly, just a second."

I've been working since I was very young—out on the courts practicing, practicing. It's a big investment of time. I'm one of the lucky ones—I got a return on my investment . . . . Money is good, money makes things happen—it's how you direct it, what you do with the money that's important. When money starts owning you, you're in trouble.

BILLIE JEAN KING
Tennis player

163

About the time we think we can make ends meet, someone moves the ends.

HERBERT HOOVER (1874-1964)
31st President of the U.S.

Beware of little expenses; a small leak will sink a great ship.

BENJAMIN FRANKLIN (1706-1790)
Statesman, scientist, and writer

PICASSO, the great painter, wanted a special piece of furniture made for a large room. He went to a cabinetmaker and, to make his wishes clear, sketched on a piece of scrap paper exactly what he wanted. When he finished, he asked what the price would be.

"No charge," said the wily craftsman, "just sign the sketch."

MOTIVATION ❖ ❖ ❖

THERE WERE TWO warring tribes . . . one that lived in the lowlands and the other high in the mountains. The mountain people invaded the lowlanders one day, and as part of their plundering of the people, they kidnapped a baby of one of the lowlander families and took the infant with them back up into the mountains.

The lowlanders didn't know how to climb the mountain. They didn't know any of the trails that the mountain people used, and they didn't know where to find the mountain people or how to track them in the steep terrain.

Even so, they sent out their best party of fighting men to climb the mountain and bring the baby home.

The men tried first one method of climbing and then another.

164

They tried one trail and then another. After several days of effort, however, they had climbed only several hundred feet.

Feeling hopeless and helpless, the lowlander men decided that the cause was lost, and they prepared to return to their village below.

As they were packing their gear for the descent, they saw the baby's mother walking toward them. They realized that she was coming down the mountain that they hadn't figured out how to climb.

And then they saw that she had the baby strapped to her back. *How could that be?*

One man greeted her and said, "We couldn't climb this mountain. How did you do this when we, the strongest and most able men in the village, couldn't do it?"

She shrugged her shoulders and said, "It wasn't your baby."

JIM STOVALL
You Don't Have to Be Blind to See
Thomas Nelson Publishers

Some people will see the light only when they feel the heat.

A MOTIVATIONAL SPEAKER tells the story about being on his return flight from giving a speech. The man sitting next to him, when learning what he did for a living, said, "Aaah, that motivational stuff doesn't last. You get yourself all pumped up for a while and then it wears off."

A passing flight attendant overheard him and said, "Well, a bath doesn't last either, but it's still a good idea."

If you think about it, food doesn't last either. Exercise doesn't last. Everything in life needs to be renewed and nurtured. We feel

165

hungry, we eat, we feel full, and in due time we get hungry again.

PAT PEARSON
You Deserve the Best
Connemara Publishers

The secret of motivation is hope.

One enterprising home builder has found a way to motivate his employees. For exceptional work he names streets after them in his housing developments.

WHEN SPANISH EXPLORER Hernando Cortés landed at Veracruz on the Gulf of Mexico in the 16th century, one of the things he did was burn his ships.

His goal was to conquer this new land by pushing west to the Pacific; by burning his ships he eliminated the possibility that his men would lose heart and sail back to Spain. The presence of the ships gave Cortés' forces an alternative if they lost the fight that lay ahead; burning the ships gave the men a powerful motive to win. Convinced that they could not turn back, they were better able to focus on the goal and do what had to be done to reach it.

Communicate everything you can to your associates. The more they know, the more they care. Once they care, there is no stopping them.

SAM WALTON (1918-1992)
Founder, Wal-Mart Corporation

A manager and a sales rep stood looking at a map on which colored pins indicated the company representative in each area.

166

"I'm not going to fire you, Wilson," the manager said, "but I'm loosening your pin a bit just to emphasize the insecurity of your situation."

"I have never found," said Harvey C. Firestone, founder of the Firestone Tire & Rubber Company, "that pay and pay alone would either bring together or hold good people. *I think it was the game itself.*"

◆ ◆ ◆ **MUSIC**

Music is one of the greatest gifts of all. It asks nothing in return but that we listen.

AN INTERVIEWER asked entertainer Victor Borge if he played any other musical instruments.

"Well, yes," replied Borge, "I have another piano."

◆ ◆ ◆ **NEGOTIATIONS**

You cannot shake hands with a clenched fist.

GOLDA MEIR (1898-1978)
Prime minister of Israel

AT A BIRTHDAY PARTY, it came time to serve the cake. A little boy named Brian blurted out, "I want the biggest piece!"

167

His mother quickly scolded him. "Brian, it's not polite to ask for the biggest piece."

The little guy looked at her in confusion, and asked, "Well then, how *do* you get it?"

OLIVE FREEMAN
in *Humor for Preaching and Teaching*
Edward K. Rowell (editor)
Baker Books

It is better to lose the saddle than the horse.

ITALIAN PROVERB

THE SIX-YEAR-OLD DAUGHTER of an accountant for a large company was used to hearing large sums of money mentioned at the dinner table. Not to be outdone, she came racing into the house one Saturday and announced to her father that she'd just sold the family dog for $10,000.

"Sold the dog!" said the father. "What are you talking about? Where's the money?"

"Oh, I didn't get any money," said the girl. "It was a trade. I got two $5,000 cats for him!"

Reconciliation is more beautiful than victory.

VIOLETA BARRIOS DE CHAMORRO
Former president of Nicaragua

❖ ❖ ❖ # NEW YEAR'S

A TOAST TO THE NEW YEAR

May you have:
Enough success to keep you eager,
Enough failure to keep you humble,
Enough joy to share with others,
Enough trials to keep you strong,
Enough hope to keep you happy,
Enough faith to banish depression,
Enough friends to give you comfort,
Enough determination to make each
day better than yesterday.

The book is closed,
The year is done,
The pages full
Of tasks begun.
A little joy,
A little care,
Along with dreams,
Are written there.
This new day brings
Another year,
Renewing hope,
Dispelling fear.
And we may find
Before the end,
A deep content,
Another friend.

ARCH WARD

NOSTALGIA ❖ ❖ ❖

Nostalgia isn't what it used to be.

PETER DE VRIES
Writer

Nostalgia is longing for a place you wouldn't move back to.

OBSTACLES ❖ ❖ ❖

To become you have to overcome.

For a long time it had seemed to me that life was about to begin—real life! But there was always some obstacle in the way, something to be gotten through first, some unfinished business . . . time to be served, a debt to be paid. Then life would begin. At last it dawned on me that these obstacles were my life.

D'SOUZA

You can't stop the waves, but you can learn to surf.

JON KABAT-ZINN
Educator and writer

The block of granite, which is an obstacle on the path of the weak, becomes a stepping-stone on the path of the strong.

THOMAS CARLYLE (1795-1881)
Scottish essayist and historian

When everything seems to be going against you, remember that the airplane takes off against the wind, not with it.

HENRY FORD (1863-1947)
Founder, Ford Motor Co.

Difficulty . . . is the nurse of greatness—a harsh nurse, who roughly rocks her foster children into strength and athletic proportion.

WILLIAM CULLEN BRYANT (1794-1878)
Poet and editor

SHE WAS OLD in years but young in spirit. Although she got around on crutches and in a wheelchair, she was a dynamo. She ran a highly successful real estate business, served on the town council, and regularly helped charitable causes in various capacities.

One day a new friend asked what had put her in the wheelchair.

"Infantile paralysis," she replied. "In the beginning, I was almost completely paralyzed."

"It's obviously still a serious disability," said the friend. "How do you cope, how do you do all the things you do?"

"Ah!" she said with a smile, "the paralysis never touched my heart or my head."

❖ ❖ ❖ **OPEN-MINDEDNESS**

Minds are like parachutes: They only work when they are open.

171

It is better to debate a question without settling it than to settle a question without debating it.

JOSEPH JOUBERT (1754-1824)
French essayist and moralist

OPPORTUNITY ♦ ♦ ♦

Killing time murders opportunities.

When the window of opportunity appears, don't pull down the shade.

TOM PETERS
Business writer and speaker

The golden opportunity you are seeking is in yourself. It is not in your environment; it is not in luck or chance, or the help of others; it is in yourself alone.

ORISON SWETT MARDEN (1848-1924)
Editor, *Success* magazine

As syndicated columnist Ann Landers has written, *"Anyone who says the days of opportunity are over is copping out."*

Every minute starts an hour and every minute is a new opportunity. Each time the clock ticks you have a chance to start over, to say, do, think, or feel something in such a way that you and the world are better for it.

WHEN THE GREAT LIBRARY of Alexandria burned, the story goes, one book was saved. But it was not a valuable book; and so a poor man, who could read a little, bought it for a few coppers. The book wasn't very interesting, but between its pages there was something very interesting indeed. It was a thin strip of vellum on which was written the secret of the "Touchstone."

The touchstone was a small pebble that could turn any common metal into pure gold. The writing explained that it was lying among thousands of other pebbles that looked exactly like it. But the secret was this: The real stone would feel warm, while ordinary pebbles are cold. So the man sold his few belongings, bought some simple supplies, camped on the seashore, and began testing pebbles.

He knew that if he picked up ordinary pebbles and threw them down again because they were cold, he might pick up the same pebble hundreds of times. So, when he felt one that was cold, he threw it into the sea. He spent a whole day doing this but none of them was the touchstone. Yet he went on and on this way. Pick up a pebble. Cold—throw it into the sea. Pick up another. Throw it into the sea.

The days stretched into weeks and the weeks into months. Yet he persisted, from morning to night. One day, however, about mid-afternoon, he picked up a pebble and it was warm. He threw it into the sea before he realized what he had done. He had formed such a strong habit of throwing each pebble into the sea that when the one he wanted came along, he still threw it away.

So it is with opportunity. Unless we are vigilant, it is easy to fail to recognize an opportunity when it is in hand and it's just as easy to throw it away.

Lack of opportunity is often nothing more than lack of purpose or direction.

LENA HIMMEL, a 16-year-old orphan, was brought from Lithuania to New York just before the turn of the century by relatives who wanted her to marry their son. But the marriage never materialized. Instead, she became a seamstress and married David Bryant, a Brooklyn jeweler, who died two years later, leaving her with a baby son.

Lena pawned the only thing of value that David had left her, a pair of diamond earrings, to put a down payment on a sewing machine. By 1904, she had done well enough to open a store on Fifth Avenue, making quality lingerie and trousseau wear for the retail and wholesale trade.

In those days, women were shy about pregnancy. One day, a young matron customer of Lena's asked her to make three dresses, all exactly the same but consecutively larger in size.

The young seamstress was horrified at such waste. She wished the woman well but told her, instead, "I'll make you a dress with an elasticized waistband that will grow with you." And she did. The first maternity dress was made, and Lane Bryant, the national chain that became synonymous with extra-sized women's clothes, was launched.

"Lena" became "Lane" when a bank teller misread her halting handwriting. Lena decided she liked the new name better, and adopted it as her own and as the name of her company.

We are all faced with great opportunities brilliantly disguised as impossible situations.

I READ THAT Antonio Stradivari made some of his most beautiful violins from a pile of broken-down, waterlogged oars he found on the docks of Venice. He was willing to connect his resources—creative vision and skillful hands—with the raw junk life offered him. From break-down, he crafted persistently until he had a new pattern: break-through.

DAWNA MARKOVA
No Enemies Within
Conari Press

When one door of happiness closes, another one opens; but often we look so long at the closed door that we do not see the one which has been opened for us.

HELEN KELLER (1880-1968)
Educator and writer

MOST PEOPLE SPEND their whole lives waiting for their "ship to come in."

Ships belong to those who can gather up a down payment, arrange financing for a tugboat to pull the ship into port, and hope there are only a few leaks when it gets there.

BRIAN ADDIS
President, Wings, Inc.

SID BERNSTEIN WORKED in the entertainment business in New York City and was also a graduate student at The New School for Social Research in Manhattan. When he took a course taught by the famous journalist Max Lerner, he was required to read a foreign newspaper every week.

For his first assignment, Bernstein read a London paper and saw a small article about a British rock group. The next week a bigger article about this British rock group was published in the paper, and the third week an even bigger article appeared. These articles motivated Bernstein to make several phone calls to London. After making the necessary business contacts, Sid

175

Bernstein got the rights to produce the first United States tour of this British rock group—The Beatles.

The people who get on in this world are the people who get up and look for the circumstances they want, and, if they can't find them, make them.

GEORGE BERNARD SHAW (1856-1950)
Irish playwright

OPTIMISM ❖ ❖ ❖

It's easy to be pleasant
When life flows like a song.

But the person worthwhile
Is the one who will smile
When everything goes dead wrong.

For the test of the heart is trouble
And it always comes with years.

And the smile that is worth
The praises of earth
Is the smile that shines through tears.

Researchers have determined that it is impossible to develop eyestrain from looking on the bright side of things.

Remember the tea kettle. Though up to its neck in hot water, it continues to sing.

176

I REALLY AM old-fashioned and square. I think there are a lot more good people in the world than bad people. I think your chances of coming out OK are better if you do what you think is right. I think that honesty is still the best policy. I think morality still pays off. I believe in all those old-fashioned things because I honestly think they work.

> ANN LANDERS
> Syndicated columnist

One of the things I learned the hard way was that it doesn't pay to get discouraged. Keeping busy and making optimism a way of life can restore your faith in yourself.

> LUCILLE BALL (1911-1989)
> Actress

Human beings are incurable optimists. They believe they have a pretty good chance to win a lottery, but that there is hardly any chance of their getting killed in a traffic accident.

Automotive genius Charles F. Kettering used to bemoan the fact that people were so quick to point out all the reasons that something wouldn't work. The person who doesn't know something can't be done, Kettering pointed out, will often find a way to go ahead and do it.

❖ ❖ ❖ PATIENCE

Patience is merely the art of concealing one's impatience.

All people commend patience, although few are willing to practice it.

PEACE ❖ ❖ ❖

When a person finds no peace within, it is useless to seek it elsewhere.

Peace, if it ever exists, will not be based on the fear of war, but on the love of peace.

HERMAN WOUK
Writer

THE SYMPTOMS OF INNER PEACE
by Jeff Rockwell

1. A tendency to think and act spontaneously rather than from fears based on past experiences.
2. An unmistakable ability to enjoy each moment.
3. A loss of interest in judging self.
4. A loss of interest in judging others.
5. A loss of interest in conflict.
6. A loss of interest in interpreting the actions of others.
7. A loss of ability to worry *(this is a very serious symptom)*.
8. Frequent, overwhelming episodes of appreciation.
9. Contented feelings of connectedness with others and nature.
10. Frequent attacks of smiling through the eyes of the heart.
11. Increasing susceptibility to love extended by others as well as the uncontrollable urge to extend it.

12. An increasing tendency to let things happen rather than to make them happen.

❖ ❖ ❖ **PERCEPTION**

Sight is a faculty; seeing is an art.

It is always better to proceed on the basis of a recognition of what is, rather than what ought to be.

STEWART ALSOP (1914-1974)
Journalist

ONE OF THE QUALITIES of successful people in all walks of life is keen observation. They notice things about people, human nature, and the general world around them. Most of us, unfortunately, go through life with our eyes half closed.

The first hint Sir Isaac Newton had leading to his important optical discoveries originated from a child's soap bubble.

The idea of printing was suggested by initials cut into the bark of a tree.

The telescope was the outcome of a boy's amusement with two pieces of glass in his father's workshop.

PERFECTION ❖ ❖ ❖

The man who insists upon seeing with perfect clearness before he decides, never decides.

HENRI FRÉDÉRIC AMIEL (1821-1881)
Swiss philosopher and writer

Only the mediocre are at their best at all times.

PERFORMING ❖ ❖ ❖

Bullfighting is as much about intuition and mental power as strength.

CHRISTINA SANCHEZ
Spanish bullfighter

SIR LAURENCE OLIVIER once gave a performance as Othello that transcended anything he had ever done. His fellow actors were stunned by it, and as he made his way to his dressing room, members of the cast lined the passageway, applauding.

He swept past them in silence and slammed the door behind him. A friend knocked and asked, "Larry, what's the problem? It was great!"

"I know it was great," he growled back, "but I don't know how I did it. So how can I be sure I can do it again?"

HELENA MODJESKA (1840-1909) was one of the most popular actresses of her time because of her emotional style and superb ability. She once gave a dramatic reading in Polish, her native tongue, at a dinner party. Her listeners, who didn't understand the language, were in tears when she finished. They didn't know it at the time, but she had just recited the Polish alphabet.

❖ ❖ ❖ PERSEVERANCE

Let me tell you the secret that has led me to my goal. My strength lies solely in my tenacity.

LOUIS PASTEUR (1822-1895)
French chemist and microbiologist

The will to persevere in the face of obstacles is often the difference between success and failure.

WHEN BETTE NESMITH worked in a Dallas bank, she was glad to have a secretarial job. She was making $300 a month, a respectable sum for 1951. But she had one problem—how to correct the errors she made on her new electric typewriter. She had some art experience and she knew that artists who work in oils just paint over errors, so she concocted a fluid to paint over her typing errors.

Before long, all the secretaries in her building were using what she then called "Mistake Out." She attempted to sell the product idea to marketing agencies and various companies (including IBM), but they turned her down. However, secretaries continued to like her product, so Bette Nesmith's kitchen became her first manufacturing facility, and she started selling it on her own.

Orders began to trickle in, and she hired a college student to help the sales effort. It wasn't easy for these two inexperienced salespeople. Dealers kept telling them that people just wouldn't paint out their mistakes. Records show that from August 1959 to April 1960, the company's total income was $1,141 and its expenses were $1,217.

But Bette didn't give up. She worked part time as a secretary, managing to buy groceries and save $200 to pay a chemist to develop a faster-drying formula.

The new formula helped. Bette Nesmith began traveling throughout the country, selling her little white bottles wherever she could. She'd arrive in a town or a city, get the local phone book, and call every local office supply dealer. She visited individual stores and would leave a dozen bottles. Orders quickened and what became the Liquid Paper Corporation began to take off.

When Bette Nesmith sold the enterprise in 1979, the tiny white bottles were earning $3.5 million annually on sales of $38 million. The buyer was the Gillette Company, and the sale price was $47.5 million.

Why is it that you always find the thing you're looking for in the last place you look?

When doubts and fears are growing,
It's hard to keep on going
From day to day not knowing
Just what the end will be.
Take each day as you find it,
If things go wrong, don't mind it,
For each day leaves behind it
A chance to start anew.

GERTRUDE ELLGAS

❖ ❖ ❖ PERSISTENCE

It takes the hammer of persistence to drive the nail of success.

JOHN MASON
Writer

Just don't give up trying to do what you really want to do. Where there's love and inspiration, I don't think you can go wrong.

ELLA FITZGERALD (1918-1996)
Singer

Trying times are not the times to stop trying.

RAY OWEN

PEOPLE WOULD ALWAYS say to my father, "Gee whiz, you've done real well. Now you can rest."

And he would reply, "Oh no. Got to keep going and do it better."

J. W. MARRIOTT, JR.
Chairman, Marriott Corporation

PARADOX

The person who
Would like to make
His dreams come true
MUST STAY AWAKE.

RICHARD WHEELER
Rotarian

Going slowly does not prevent arriving.

NIGERIAN PROVERB

Our greatest glory consists not in never falling, but in rising every time we fall.

OLIVER GOLDSMITH (1730-1774)
British writer

WHEN CAL RIPKEN, JR., the Baltimore Orioles' all-star shortstop, was chasing Lou Gehrig's record for the most baseball games played consecutively, he was asked if he ever went to the ballpark with a lot of aches and pains. Ripken said, "Yeah, just about every day."

Though Ripken's casual reply makes it sound routine, overcoming everyday aches and pains without fail for 13 years is a remarkable achievement for an athlete—or for anyone else for that matter. Throughout his long and distinguished career, Ripken has encountered the same daily challenges and setbacks as his fellow players and has risen above them all. His dedication, drive, and youthful energy and enthusiasm have proven all but inexhaustible.

What's the secret behind Cal Ripken's incredible longevity and success in a career as demanding as professional baseball? One of the keys to his success must surely be that he has conditioned himself to be comfortable being uncomfortable.

ROB GILBERT
Editor, *Bits & Pieces*

THE IMPORTANT THING is to stick to it. As American journalist Jacob A. Riis once said: "When nothing seems to help, I go and look at the stonecutter hammering away at his rock, perhaps a hundred times without as much as a crack showing in it. Yet, at the hundred and first blow it will split in two, and I know it was not that last blow that did it, but all that had gone before."

JOHN H. MENNEAR
Teacher and writer

The world has a lot of starters but very few finishers.

When you get into a tight place and everything goes against you, until it seems as though you cannot hang on a minute longer, never give up then, for that is just the place and time that the tide will turn.

HARRIET BEECHER STOWE (1811-1896)
Writer

WHEN A.J. CRONIN retired as a London doctor because of ill health, he moved to a quiet farming community in Scotland. There Cronin hoped to start a new career as a novelist, a dream he had had since childhood.

For months he worked in a small attic room, filling tablet after tablet with handwritten text, and sending it off to a London secretarial bureau to be typed. Finally the first typed chapters were returned in the mail. He picked them up eagerly, anxious to get a fresh impression of what he had written.

As Cronin read the manuscript, his disgust mounted. How could he have written such terrible material? He was a failure already—with his first book only half written. He stomped out into the drizzling rain for a lonely walk, throwing the manuscript onto an ash pile beside the house.

Crossing the heath, he met a neighbor, an old farmer, digging a drainage ditch in a boggy field. The farmer inquired how Cronin's writing was coming along. When Cronin reported what he had done with his manuscript, the old farmer was silent for several minutes. Then he spoke.

"No doubt you're the one that's right, and I'm the one that's wrong. My father ditched this bog all his days and never made a pasture. I've dug it all my days and I've never made a pasture. But pasture or no pasture, I cannot help but dig. For my father knew, and I know, that if you only dig enough, a pasture can be made here."

Ashamed of himself, Cronin walked back to the house, picked the manuscript out of the ashes, and dried it out in the oven. Then he went back to work, writing and rewriting until it satisfied him. The book was *Hatter's Castle*, the first in a long string of successful novels.

Life is like riding a bicycle. You don't fall off unless you stop pedaling.

CLAUDE PEPPER (1900-1989)
U.S. congressman

Rule #1: Take one more step.

Rule #2: When you don't think you can take one more step, refer to Rule #1.

H. JACKSON BROWN, JR.
Writer

186

❖ ❖ ❖ PERSPECTIVE

A MAN WAS MISSING his ax. He suspected his neighbor's young son. The boy looked like a thief, acted like a thief, and spoke like a thief.

When the man eventually found his misplaced ax, his neighbor's son looked, acted, and spoke like any other young boy.

The dark moment the caterpillar calls the end of the world is the sun-filled moment the butterfly calls the beginning.

Nothing increases the size of a fish like fishing all by yourself.

THE PRESIDENT of a television network summoned the vice president in charge of human resources. "I want to fire that woman in the little office down at the end of the hall," he commanded. "I've been watching her for the past two weeks, and all she does from morning to night is look out of the window."

"Wait a minute," said the HR executive. "That's our vice president in charge of new ideas. That new police drama that everybody loves, the new game show that's cleaning up millions, those new situation comedies—she thought them up looking out the window."

"In that case," said the president, reaching for his phone, "let's have somebody up here to wash her window!"

TWO BUCKETS were on their way to the well. "You look mighty sad," said one bucket to the other.

"I was just thinking about the futility of what we do," said the sad bucket. "Time after time we go down to the well and get full, but we always come back to the well empty."

"You've got the wrong slant," said the other bucket. "I enjoy what we're doing. The way I look at it, no matter how many times we come to the well empty, we always come away full."

If dandelions were hard to grow, they would be most welcome on any lawn.

ANDREW MASON

In times like these, it helps to remember that there have always been times like these.

A PROMINENT PSYCHOLOGIST used to start his lectures this way: He would appear on the platform with a large piece of white card-board with a small black dot in the lower left-hand corner, then ask someone in the audience what they saw.

Back came the usual answer. They saw a small black dot in the lower left-hand corner.

"What you saw is what you chose to see," the psychologist would then say. "You could have said that what you saw was a large empty white space—enough in which to copy Lincoln's Gettysburg Address, the Ten Commandments, or the Bill of Rights."

The point he was leading up to is that it is not what happens to us that is so important as the way we see it, and that the choice is ours.

He would then go on to tell the true story of one Henry Fawcett, an Englishman. This young man accompanied his father on a hunting trip. The father accidently discharged his shotgun, blinding his son in both eyes. The boy was just 20 years old at the time.

Before the accident, the son had been a bright, ambitious young man with a great future. No one would have blamed him if the accident had made him bitter and full of despair. And that was how it did seem to him at first. But there was one thing that saved him: He had deeply loved his father and knew that his father was nearly out of his mind with grief at what he had done to his son.

The only way he could save his father's sanity was to choose hope over despair himself. And that is just what he did. He pretended to take an interest in life that he did not feel. He pretended to have hope that he could be a useful citizen, though he himself felt no such hope.

Then an odd thing happened. The pretense turned into reality. It was as if, by an act of will, he had exorcised an evil spirit, driving it out of himself. The result: Henry Fawcett was elected to Parliament. Later, he became postmaster general, where he brought about great improvements in the English postal and telegraph systems.

By deliberately altering his attitude, he carved out a useful career and found a good life for himself, mastering his fate. He chose, by a sheer act of will, to see the white space, not the small black dot.

TWO FREIGHT TRAINS collided, and a young man named Westinghouse set to work to prevent a repetition of such an accident. The result was the invention of the air brake and the growth of a great industry.

Railroad executives had the attitude of Commodore Vanderbilt who, when George Westinghouse explained his invention, exclaimed, "Do you mean to tell me that you expect to stop a train with wind? I have no time to waste on damn fools."

Westinghouse was aware of the basic problem of the air brake: If the compressed air system failed, there was no way to stop the train. By reversing his approach to the problem, he finally came up with a solution: Heavy springs held the train's brakes on, and the compressed air pushed the brakes away from the wheels. If the air system malfunctioned, the springs clamped the brakes back against the wheels, and the train came to a safe stop.

By looking at his problem from a different angle, Westinghouse was able to perfect the air brake, which was adopted by the entire industry.

Losers visualize the penalties of failure. Winners visualize the rewards of success.

ROB GILBERT
Editor, *Bits & Pieces*

Angels can fly because they take themselves lightly.

G.K. CHESTERTON (1874-1936)
English writer

The world really isn't much worse than it ever was. It's just that the news coverage is so much better.

A LOAF OF BREAD fell from a bakery truck and, as it hit the pavement, a crumb broke off. Three sparrows swooped down on the crumb and began fighting over it. One bird finally succeeded in flying off with the crumb, the two others in close pursuit. A series of frenzied aerial maneuvers followed until the crumb was at last consumed by one of the birds.

The loaf was untouched. Only the crumb had seemed worth

the fight. If the birds had displayed more vision and less greed, they could have all been satisfied.

People, like birds, quarrel over trivialities. In the heat of the struggle, life's bigger, more enriching prizes escape them.

Psychologists say that if you ask people to write down on a piece of paper all their personality strengths, they will come up with only five or six. Asked to do the same for their weaknesses, the list will be two or three times as long.

❖ ❖ ❖ PESSIMISM

There's many a pessimist who got that way by financing an optimist.

The person who is sure nothing can be done is usually someone who has never done anything.

To GUARD AGAINST the tendency to say "no" too quickly, one executive keeps the following sign on his wall:

HOW TO BURY A GOOD IDEA

It will never work.
We've never done it that way before.
We're doing fine without it.
We can't afford it.
We're not ready for it.
It's not our responsibility.

PETS ❖ ❖ ❖

You can learn these things from your dog: to love children, to drink plenty of water, to be a dependable friend, to express pleasure when treated well, to guard faithfully the interests of those who care for you, and to be faithful until death.

"I WANT A DOG of which I can be proud," said Mrs. Newlyrich. "Does that one have a good pedigree?"

"Oh, yes," declared the kennel owner, "if he could talk, he wouldn't speak to either of us."

JACOB MORTON BRAUDE
Braude's Treasury of Wit and Humor
Prentice Hall

PLANNING ❖ ❖ ❖

"IT IS A POPULAR conception that to make rapid fundamental progress it is only necessary to concentrate large quantities of men and money on a problem," said Charles Kettering, the inventor.

"Years ago when we were developing the first electrically operated cash register I ran into this type of thinking. My boss was going to Europe and wanted the job finished before he took off.

" 'Give Kettering twice as many men so he can finish it up in half the time.' When I objected to this idea, he asked, 'Why can't you? If 10 men can dig 10 rods of ditch in a day, then surely 20 men can dig 20 rods.'

"I replied, 'Do you think if one hen can hatch a setting of eggs in three weeks, two hens can hatch a setting in a week and a half? This is more a job of hatching eggs than digging ditches.' "

192

❖ ❖ ❖ POTENTIAL

To be what we are, and to become what we are capable of becoming, is the only end of life.

ROBERT LOUIS STEVENSON (1850-1894)
Scottish writer

A FAVORITE FISH of many hobbyists is the Japanese carp, commonly known as the *koi*. The fascinating thing about the *koi* is that if you keep it in a small fish bowl, it will only grow to be two or three inches long. Place the *koi* in a larger tank or small pond and it will reach six to 10 inches. Put it in a large pond and it may get as long as a foot and a half. However, when placed in a huge lake where it can really stretch out, it has the potential to reach sizes up to three feet.

You've probably already figured out the simple point to this illustration. The size of the fish is in direct relation to the size of the pond.

A comparable analogy can be made concerning people. Our growth is determined by the size of our world. Of course, it is not the world's measurable dimensions that are important, but the mental, emotional, spiritual, and physical opportunities we expose ourselves to.

Realizing that growth comes from the inside and not the outside, we come to the realization that unless we expand who we are, we'll always have what we've got.

GLENN VAN EKEREN
Speaker's Sourcebook II
Prentice Hall

Anyone can count the seeds in an apple.
No one can count the apples in a seed.

EACH SECOND we live is a new and unique moment of the universe, a moment that will never be again . . . . And what do we teach our children? We teach them that two and two make four, and that Paris is the capital of France.

When will we also teach them what they are?

We should say to each of them: Do you know what you are? You are a marvel. You are unique. In all the years that have passed, there has never been another child like you. Your legs, your arms, your clever fingers, the way you move.

You may become a Shakespeare, a Michelangelo, a Beethoven. You have the capacity for anything. Yes, you are a marvel. And when you grow up, can you then harm another who is, like you, a marvel?

You must work—we must all work—to make the world worthy of its children.

PABLO CASALS (1876-1973)
Spanish cellist, conductor, and composer

The most delightful surprise in life is to suddenly recognize your own worth.

MAXWELL MALTZ (1899-1975)
Surgeon and writer

AN AMERICAN INDIAN tells about a brave who found an eagle's egg and put it into the nest of a prairie chicken. The eaglet hatched with the brood of chicks and grew up with them.

All its life, the changeling eagle, thinking it was a prairie chicken, did what the prairie chickens did. It scratched in the dirt for seeds and insects to eat. It clucked and cackled. And it flew in a brief thrashing of wings and flurry of feathers no more than a few feet off the ground. After all, that's how prairie chickens were supposed to fly.

194

Years passed. And the changeling eagle grew very old. One day, it saw a magnificent bird far above in the cloudless sky. Hanging with graceful majesty on the powerful wind currents, it soared with scarcely a beat of its strong golden wings.

"What a beautiful bird!" said the changeling eagle to its neighbor. "What is it?"

"That's an eagle—the chief of the birds," the neighbor clucked. "But don't give it a second thought. You could never be like him."

So the changeling eagle never gave it another thought. And it died thinking it was a prairie chicken.

THE CHRISTOPHERS

Some people dream of worthy accomplishments while others stay awake and do them.

D.W. Griffith, the noted film director, once received a letter from a fan requesting an autograph. Griffith wrote back, *"Stop collecting autographs and start doing something that will make your autograph worth collecting."*

PAUL HARTUNIAN
Rare documents expert

In every child who is born, in no matter what circumstances, and no matter what parents, the potentiality of the human race is born again.

JAMES AGEE (1909-1955)
Writer

. . . [E]very rule in the book can be broken, except one—be who you are, and become all you were meant to be . . . .

SYDNEY J. HARRIS (1917-1986)
Syndicated columnist

Rebellion against your handicaps gets you nowhere. Self-pity gets you nowhere. One must have the adventurous daring to accept oneself as a bundle of possibilities and undertake the most interesting game in the world—making the most of one's best.

HARRY EMERSON FOSDICK (1878-1969)
Religious leader

Life is like a 10-speed bike. Most of us have gears we never use.

There is a vitality, a life force, an energy, a quickening that is translated through you into action and because there is only one of you in all time, this expression is unique. And if you block it, it will never exist through any other medium and it will be lost. The world will not have it.

MARTHA GRAHAM (1894-1991)
Dancer and choreographer

My mother said to me, "If you become a soldier, you'll be a general; if you become a monk, you'll end up as Pope." Instead, I became a painter and wound up as Picasso.

PABLO PICASSO (1881-1973)
Spanish painter and sculptor

DANTE GABRIEL ROSSETTI, the famous 19th-century poet and artist, was once approached by an elderly man. The old fellow had some sketches and drawings that he wanted Rossetti to look at and tell him if they were any good, or if they, at least, showed potential talent.

Rossetti looked them over carefully. After the first few he knew that they were worthless, showing not the least sign of artistic talent. But Rossetti was a kind man and he told the elderly man as gently as possible that the pictures were without much value and showed little talent. He was sorry, but he could not lie to the man.

The visitor was disappointed, but seemed to expect Rossetti's judgment. He then apologized for taking up Rossetti's time, but would he just look at a few more drawings—these done by a young art student?

Rossetti looked over the second batch of sketches and immediately became enthused about the talent they revealed. "These," he said, "ah, these are good. This young man, whoever he is, has great talent. He should be given every help and encouragement in his career as an artist. He has a great future, if he will work hard and stick with it."

Rossetti could see that the old fellow was deeply moved. "Who is this fine young artist?" he asked. "Your son?"

"No," said the old fellow sadly. "It is me—40 years ago. If only I had heard your praise then. For you see, I got discouraged and gave up—too soon.

———————————

A TOURIST WENT into a jewelry shop in Hong Kong, and was shown a series of precious stones. Among them was a dull stone, completely lacking in luster.

"That's certainly not beautiful," said the tourist.

"Wait," said the jeweler. He took the stone from the tray and closed his fist over it. Moments later, he opened his fist and the stone glowed with beauty. "This is an opal," the jeweler explained. "It's what we call a sympathetic jewel. It needs only to be gripped with the human hand to bring out its radiance and beauty."

PRAYER ❖ ❖ ❖

After saying your prayers at night, you have to get up the next day and do something to try to make them come true.

A man in a large eastern U.S. city wrote to the local newspaper to report that the country was in far worse shape than most people suspected. His evidence: *"Every time I call Dial-a-Prayer I get a busy signal."*

If your troubles are deep-seated and of long standing, try kneeling.

A LITTLE GIRL was about to undergo an operation and the surgeon explained that before he could make her well, he would have to put her to sleep.

"All right," said the little girl, "but first I have to say my prayers." Then she began, "Now I lay me down to sleep . . . ."

All went well, but that night the surgeon got down on his knees and prayed for the first time in 35 years.

A MINISTER had earned a vacation from his congregation, and he decided to make it a golfing holiday. He went to a golfing resort, and on his first day out on the course, he learned that Arnold Palmer played the course frequently.

The toughest hole was the 17th, and as the clergyman approached the tee his caddie said, "When Arnold Palmer plays this hole, he uses a No. 3 iron and says a little prayer."

"I'll give it a try," said the clergyman. But the ball landed in a sand trap. "Ah, well," he said, "I guess the good Lord didn't hear me."

"He probably heard you," said the caddie, "but when Mr. Palmer says his prayer, he keeps his head down."

❖ ❖ ❖ **PREDICTIONS**

Fearless forecast, quoted in *The Wall Street Journal*: "Oil prices will go up or down, more or less, unless there are some unforeseen circumstances."

We have two classes of forecasters: Those who don't know—and those who don't know they don't know.

JOHN KENNETH GALBRAITH
Economist

❖ ❖ ❖ **PREPARATION**

THE BEST SPEAKERS know enough to be scared.

"Stagefright is the sweat of perfection," said television journalist Edward R. Murrow.

"The only difference between the pros and the novices is that the pros have trained the butterflies to fly in formation," said fellow broadcast journalist Edwin Newman.

What's the best medicine to keep stagefright from becoming disaster? In a word: Preparation.

To give yourself the best possible chance of playing to your potential, you must prepare for every eventuality. That means practice. Now I know that very often you "just don't have the time." In spite of that, if you really want to improve, you will have to make the *decision,* and then the *commitment.* There are no shortcuts. You must lay the proper foundation.

SEVE BALLESTEROS
Spanish professional golfer

Before you decide about your aim in life, check your ammunition.

FOR 33 YEARS, Red Barber broadcast baseball games. One reason for his success was his habit of thorough preparation before each game. "You have to be as fully prepared for the dull game as you are for the great one," said Barber, "or else you won't be prepared for the great one."

It's better to be prepared for an opportunity and not have one than to have an opportunity and not be prepared.

WHITNEY YOUNG (1921-1971)
Civil rights leader

❖ ❖ ❖ PRIORITIES

Anything less than a conscious commitment to the important is
an unconscious commitment to the unimportant.

STEPHEN R. COVEY
First Things First
Simon & Schuster

**Henry Doherty, founder of the Cities Service Oil Company, used
to say that the hardest thing to find, when hiring someone, was
the ability to concentrate on what was important.**

❖ ❖ ❖ PROBLEMS

THERE'S AN OLD STORY out of the American West about how cattle
act in winter storms.

Sometimes the storms took a heavy toll. They would start
with freezing rains. Temperatures would plummet below zero.
Then, bitterly cold winds would begin to pile up huge snowdrifts.
Most cattle turned their backs to the icy blasts and they would
begin to move downwind until they came up against the
inevitable barbed wire fence. In the big storms, they would pile up
against the fence and die by the score.

But one breed always survived. Herefords would instinctively head into the wind. They would stand shoulder to shoulder,
heads down, facing the blasts.

As one cowboy once put it, "You most always found the
Herefords alive and well. I guess that's the greatest lesson I ever
learned on the prairies—just face life's storms."

201

For every problem
Under the sun

There is a solution
Or there is none.

If there's a solution
Go and find it.

If there isn't,
Never mind it.

One of the nice things about problems is that a good many of them do not exist except in our imagination.

STEVE ALLEN
Entertainer

PROBLEMS—in the family, at work or elsewhere—are seldom fun. In seeking solutions, we might ask ourselves questions like these:

Do I keep an open mind to all proposals? Or do I block out some because of my own dislikes?

Am I willing to work out a fair compromise? Or do I insist on having things my own way?

Am I genuinely pleased when somebody else comes up with a bright idea? Or do I regard it as a personal affront?

Have I such a clear picture of the goal that I can distinguish a sensible compromise and an unworthy surrender?

FATHER JAMES KELLER (1900-1977)
Founder, The Christophers

A DOZEN discontented figures in a community once visited a wise man, clamoring to tell him their problems.

"Each of you write your biggest problem down on a piece of paper," said the wise man, "and six of you stand here to my right and six to my left. Now exchange papers and you will have a new trouble to fret about."

The malcontents complied. Within a minute, all were clamoring to have their own troubles back!

As someone once said, "The best way out of a problem is through it."

AFTER STARRING in *Under Western Stars*, his first movie, Roy Rogers started to receive overwhelming stacks of fan mail. Rogers faithfully began the task of answering the mail. Making $150 a week, however, he couldn't even pay for the postage.

Finally he went to Herb Yates, head of Republic Pictures, and told him about the problem, hoping that the studio would handle some of the fan mail. Yates wasted little time telling Rogers that he was foolish to worry about answering fan mail; nobody else in the business did, because it took too much time and money.

Rogers couldn't accept that. He felt that if someone was thoughtful enough to sit down and write him a letter, he had an obligation to answer it.

Much in demand, Rogers used his popularity to help solve the problem. He arranged a series of personal appearances and used the money he earned, often more than his weekly salary at Republic Pictures, to help defray his mailing expenses. For the first two years at Republic, the cost of handling his fan mail exceeded the salary the studio was paying him.

Rogers traveled thousands of miles and performed countless

one-night stands to buy stamps, purchase pictures, and pay the salaries of four people he hired to help answer the fan mail. And he became one of Hollywood's most popular and longest-lived stars. *Every problem has a solution.*

PROCRASTINATION ❖ ❖ ❖

He who hesitates is last.

MAE WEST (1892-1980)
Actress

There is no pleasure in having nothing to do; the fun is in having lots to do and not doing it.

MARY WILSON LITTLE

THEY WERE GOING to be all that they wanted to be—tomorrow.

None would be braver or kinder than they—tomorrow.

A friend who was troubled and weary, they knew, would be glad of a lift—and needed it too. On him they would call—see what they could do—tomorrow.

Each morning they stacked up the letters they'd write—tomorrow.

The greatest of people they just might have been,

The world would have opened its heart to them.

But in fact, they passed on and faded from view,

And all that they left when their living was through

Was a mountain of things they intended to do—tomorrow.

THE FOUR-LETTER SOLUTION TO PROCRASTINATION

DOn't waIT

Mañana is often the busiest day of the week.

SPANISH PROVERB

Most of us spend half our time wishing for things we could have if we didn't spend half our time wishing.

ALEXANDER WOOLLCOTT (1887-1943)
Writer

❖ ❖ ❖ PROFESSIONALISM

ALMOST EVERYONE knows that Hank Aaron broke Babe Ruth's long-standing home run record in baseball, but almost no one knows that Hank Aaron's record was broken by Sadaharu Oh of the Japanese leagues.

In his inspiring autobiography *A Zen Way of Baseball*, Sadaharu Oh, arguably the greatest home-run hitter of all time, tells of his thoughts in the locker room before the last game of his playing career:

"I am a professional ballplayer, I told myself. A professional. The word has meaning for me as few others in my vocabulary do.

"There is a standard of performance you must maintain. It is the best you are able to give and then more—and to maintain that at a level of consistency. No excuses for the demands of your ego or the extremes of your emotions. It is an inner thing.

"I held myself to that standard for 22 years. It is my proudest achievement."

Professionals are people who can do their job when they don't feel like it. Amateurs are people who can't do their job when they do feel like it.

ON FEBRUARY 15, 1985, every theater on Broadway darkened its lights at curtain time to honor Ethel Merman. The 75-year-old dynamo, who became a legend in her own time though she never had a singing lesson, had died earlier that day.

Said one actor who had worked with her, "We'll never see a presence on stage like that again."

Two things about Ethel Merman come to mind. One was her tremendous confidence in her own ability. Once, after being asked if she had ever been frightened about performing, she replied: "Why should I be scared? I know my lines."

And then there was the tremendous dedication she brought to all of her roles. "When I do a show," she once said, "I sort of take the veil. No cocktail parties, no dinner parties. The show revolves around me and a lot of people are depending on me."

Three Minutes a Day
Volume 24, Christopher Books

PROGRESS ❖ ❖ ❖

The art of progress is to preserve order amid change and to preserve change amid order.

ALFRED NORTH WHITEHEAD (1861-1947)
English mathematician and philosopher

Our company has, indeed, *stumbled* onto some of its new products.

206

But never forget that you can only stumble if you're moving.

RICHARD P. CARLTON
Former CEO, 3M Corporation

If there is no struggle, there is no progress.

FREDERICK DOUGLASS (1817-1895)
Abolitionist

All change is not growth; all movement is not forward.

ELLEN GLASGOW (1873-1945)
Novelist

❖ ❖ ❖ **PROMISES**

ARE YOU a "probability" or a "promise"? There's a BIG difference.

Listen to yourself when you speak. Are you more likely to say "I'll probably do that," or "I promise I'll do that"?

In all probability, if you say you'll probably do something— you probably won't. When you use the words "I promise," there's a whole different level of commitment and accountability.

The words you use are a "preview of coming attractions." If you want to become more productive, change your "probablys" to "promises."

The person who is slowest in making a promise is most faithful in its performance.

JEAN-JACQUES ROUSSEAU (1712-1778)
French philosopher and writer

QUALITY ❖ ❖ ❖

The bitterness of poor quality remains long after the sweetness of a *low price* is forgotten.

---

*The bitterness of poor quality remains long after the sweetness of **meeting the schedule** has been forgotten.*

THE CRAFTSMAN'S SECRET

SEVERAL YEARS have gone by now since the day I learned the craftsman's secret. I was in Milan, writing an article on the great tailors, shirtmakers, and bootmakers that still thrived in Italy. My first stop was at a small shop in the center of town, a shop famous throughout Europe for the luxurious quality and superior cut of its handmade shirts.

I introduced myself to the owner, an immaculately groomed gentleman in his mid-50s, soft-spoken and terribly gracious. He showed me fabrics that would never have entered my most sybaritic fantasies.

The cut was a full poem: full without being sloppy, sleeves that tapered gently to the trim cuff, classic short- and long-point collars with just the exact amount of tie space for the knot. There was that sense of simplicity that only the purist really appreciates. Need I add, prices were commensurate.

While we were talking, I noticed out of the corner of my eye an elderly gentleman, white-haired and bespectacled, sitting on a high stool in front of a draughting-type table in the corner. My host caught my look. "That's my father," he smiled. "Perhaps you would care to meet him?"

He introduced us, and I asked how long he had been cutting shirts. The son replied that his father had learned the art sitting on his father's knees, and as it happened, last week he had just celebrated his 84th birthday.

Might I presume to know, I said, what was his secret for being able to make such beautiful shirts? Is it, I wanted to know, that he has experience and the gift for it?

The son translated, and the father smiled and spoke slowly for a minute or two.

"My father says that you must excuse him, but he has no technical answer to the question. He says the experience is very important, and he is not sure about 'the gift' because shirt-making is all he has ever done. But he says that to make a beautiful shirt you just don't cut with the knife, you cut the cloth *with love*. My father is something of a poet, yes?"

To be sure. But it was the answer, nevertheless. As Thomas Carlyle blatantly put it, "There is practically nothing in this world that some man cannot make a little worse and sell a little cheaper—and he who considers only the price is that man's lawful prey."

The elderly gentleman knew very well the difference between art and industry. You care about what you are doing: *That's the craftman's secret!*

From *Louis of Boston* catalogue

AN OLD JANITOR named Eltjo Zomer had become a legend around the company by the time he retired. Some years ago at a farewell party his friends threw for him, his supervisor recalled how Eltjo, who had recently arrived in the United States from The Netherlands, recoiled when he first glimpsed the messy floors, greasy machines, and flyspecked windows he would be responsible for. But Eltjo just shrugged his shoulders and dug in.

In those days a little dirt in the plant was accepted as a necessary part of production. So whenever Eltjo came down the aisle with his broom, the workers would josh him and purposely toss dirt behind the industrious sweeper. Before long, however, in spite of these setbacks, the department took on an unaccustomed gleam.

Then one day the company president walked through the department. He was so impressed with its cleanliness compared with other parts of the plant that he got hold of an interpreter and personally congratulated Eltjo.

From then on, everyone in the department helped Eltjo to keep the place tidy. The practice spread to other departments. As the surroundings became more pleasant and orderly, employees found themselves not only enjoying their work more, but also doing more work, and doing it better than before.

In such a simple way, the sweeper's broom became a contributor to quality.

We're all sweepers to some extent. The orderliness that we establish for our own endeavors is the first essential for quality work and the resulting quality product.

It is the willingness of people to give of themselves over and above the demands of the job that distinguishes the great from the merely adequate organization.

PETER F. DRUCKER
Management consultant

QUESTIONS ❖ ❖ ❖

Sometimes it is better to ask some of the questions than to know all the answers.

The question should never be who is right, but what is right.

GLEN GARDINER

❖ ❖ ❖ REDUNDANCY

AN EXECUTIVE had a reputation for never throwing anything away, especially correspondence dating back years. The secretary, cramped for filing space, one day asked to dispose of some of the older, more useless material. The executive was reluctant, but finally said, *"Well, all right, but be sure you make a copy of everything before you do."*

———

THE U.S. NAVY tried to find out which of its millions of paperwork forms were superfluous.

The personnel department immediately issued a "Paperwork Necessity Inquiry Form."

❖ ❖ ❖ REGRET

Regret for the things we did can be tempered by time; it is regret for the things we did not do that is inconsolable.

SYDNEY J. HARRIS (1917-1986)
Syndicated columnist

———

Three things never return: the past, the neglected opportunity, and the spoken word.

———

RELAXATION ❖ ❖ ❖

You can't look at a sleeping cat and be tense.

JANE PAULEY
Television personality

Here's a marvelous, economical idea for a vacation trip: Climb into a hammock and let your mind wander.

RESILIENCE ❖ ❖ ❖

THE LATE EARL NIGHTINGALE, writer and publisher of inspirational and motivational material, once told a story about a boy named Sparky. For Sparky, school was all but impossible. He failed every subject in the eighth grade. He flunked physics in high school, getting a grade of zero.

Sparky also flunked Latin, algebra, and English. He didn't do much better in sports. Although he did manage to make the school's golf team, he promptly lost the only important match of the season. There was a consolation match; he lost that too.

Throughout his youth, Sparky was awkward socially. He was not actually disliked by the other students; no one cared that much. He was astonished if a classmate ever said hello to him outside of school hours.

There's no way to tell how he might have done at dating. Sparky never once asked a girl to go out in high school. He was too afraid of being turned down.

Sparky was a loser. He, his classmates . . . everyone knew it. So he rolled with it. Sparky had made up his mind early in life that if things were meant to work out, they would. Otherwise he would content himself with what appeared to be his inevitable mediocrity.

However, one thing was important to Sparky—drawing. He was proud of his artwork. Of course, no one else appreciated it. In his senior year of high school, he submitted some cartoons to the editors of the yearbook. The cartoons were turned down. Despite this particular rejection, Sparky was so convinced of his ability that he decided to become a professional artist.

After completing high school, he wrote a letter to Walt Disney Studios. He was told to send some samples of his artwork, and the subject for a cartoon was suggested. Sparky drew the proposed cartoon. He spent a great deal of time on it and on all the other drawings he submitted. Finally, the reply came from Disney Studios. He had been rejected once again. *Another loss for the loser.*

So Sparky decided to write his own autobiography in cartoons. He described his childhood self—a little boy loser and chronic underachiever. The cartoon character would soon become famous worldwide.

For Sparky, the boy who had such lack of success in school and whose work was rejected again and again, was Charles Schulz. He created the "Peanuts" comic strip and the little cartoon character whose kite would never fly and who never succeeded in kicking a football—Charlie Brown.

———

WHEN HARD TIMES come and life seems to be bowling you over, remember this story from *The Pastor's Story File*, published by Sarasota Press in Platteville, Colorado:

A father took his boy into a toy shop. The boy got away from his dad and found a statue of a man made of balloons. The boy looked at it for a minute, and then he drew back his fist and hit the balloon man just as hard as he could. The man fell over, and then popped right back up.

The confused boy backed off and looked at him again and then backed up and then hit him again as hard as he could. Again the man fell over, and again he popped right back up.

The boy's father walked around the corner and saw his son hit the balloon man. The father asked his son, "Why do you think he comes back up when you hit him and knock him down?"

The boy thought for a minute and said, "I don't know, I guess it's because he's standing up on the inside."

A champion is one who gets up even when he can't.

JACK DEMPSEY (1895-1983)
Former heavyweight boxing champion

SOMEONE ONCE asked Paul Harvey, the radio commentator, to reveal the secret of his success.

"I get up when I fall down," said Harvey.

RESPONSIBILITY ❖ ❖ ❖

PEOPLE ARE INCLINED, when in the wrong, to lay the blame on someone else. We're like the small boy who was standing on the cat's tail. His mother, hearing the terrible commotion, called from an adjoining room: "Tommy, stop pulling that cat's tail!"

"I'm not pulling the cat's tail. I'm standing on it. He's the one that's doing the pulling."

214

It is our responsibilities, not ourselves, that we should take seriously.

One trouble with the world is that so many people who stand up vigorously for their rights fall down miserably on their duties.

♦ ♦ ♦ **RISK**

To laugh is to risk appearing the fool.
To weep is to risk appearing sentimental.
To reach out for another is to risk involvement.
To expose feelings is to risk exposing your true self.
To place your ideas, your dreams, before a crowd
    is to risk their loss.
To love is to risk not being loved in return.
To live is to risk dying.
To hope is to risk failure.
But risks must be taken.
Because the greatest hazard in life is to risk nothing.
If you risk nothing and do nothing, you dull your spirit.
You may avoid suffering and sorrow,
But you cannot learn, feel, change, grow, love, and live.
Chained by your attitude, you are a slave.
You have forfeited your freedom.
Only if you risk are you free.

Before the beginning of great brilliance, there must be chaos.

Before a brilliant person begins something great, he must look foolish to the crowd.

I CHING

215

There was a very cautious man
Who never laughed or played.

He never risked, he never tried,
He never sang or prayed.

And when he one day passed away.
His insurance was denied.

For since he never really lived,
They claimed he never died.

Nobody can go back and start a new beginning, but anyone can start today and make a new *ending*.

MARIA ROBINSON
Motivational speaker

It's better to be a lion for a day than a sheep all your life.

SISTER ELIZABETH KENNY (1880-1952)
Australian nurse

RUMORS ❖ ❖ ❖

Trying to squash a rumor is like trying to unring a bell.

SHANA ALEXANDER
Journalist

A MAN once asked a wise philosopher how he could make amends for falsely accusing a friend. The philosopher told him to put a goose feather on each doorstep in his town.

The next day the philosopher said, "Now go and collect the feathers."

"It can't be done," cried the man. "The wind blew all night, and the feathers have scattered everywhere."

"Exactly," said the sage, "and so it is with the reckless words you spoke against your neighbor."

———

THE PRESIDENT of a fast-growing company called his public relations vice president to his office one day and said, "Somebody is trying to buy our company, and if they succeed, you and I will be out on our ears. I want you to do something that will get the price of our stock up so that it'll be too expensive for them to acquire us. I don't care what you have to do to bring this about; whatever it is, just do it!"

Within two days the stock rose 14 points, and the president was delighted.

"What in the world did you do?" he asked the vice president of public relations.

"Simple," she said. "I started a rumor, and Wall Street liked it."

"What was the rumor?"

"I told them you were leaving the company," she said.

♦ ♦ ♦ **SALES**
═══════════════════════

THE WORLD'S SHORTEST SALES COURSE

#1. Know their business.
#2. Know your stuff.

———

Columbus was definitely the world's most amazing salesman. He started out not knowing where ~~it was going. When he got there~~ he didn't know where it was, s~~ And when he got back he couldn't say~~ where he'd been. And he did i ~~all on borrowed money—and he got 2~~ got a repeat order.

HARRY BULLIS, former chairman of the board of General Mills, used to give his salespeople the following advice: "Forget about the sales you hope to make and concentrate on the service you want to render."

The moment people's attention is centered on service to others, they become more dynamic, more forceful and harder to resist. How can you resist someone who is trying to help you solve a problem?

Mr. Bullis said he would tell his salespeople "that if they would start out each morning with the thought, 'I want to help as many people as possible today,' instead of 'I want to make as many sales as possible today,' they would find a more easy and open approach to their buyers, and they would make more sales. He who goes out to help his fellowman to a happier and easier way of life is exercising the highest type of salesmanship."

A GREAT PROPHET once addressed a herd of donkeys.

"What would a donkey require for a three-day journey?" the prophet asked.

And they answered, "Six bundles of hay and three bags of dates."

"I cannot give six bundles of hay and three bags of dates," the great prophet said. "Who will go for less?"

One donkey said he could go for six bundles of hay and two bags of dates. Another offered to make the journey for three bundles of hay and one bag of dates. Then one long-eared, sad-looking donkey said he would go for just one bundle of hay.

"Thou art a disgrace to the herd and an ass," said the prophet. "Thou cannot live for three days on one bundle of hay, much less undertake the journey to make profit."

"True," replied the donkey, hanging his long ears in shame. "But I wanted to get the order."

A YOUNG life insurance sales agent walked into a factory and asked to see the sales manager. When the manager finally greeted her in his office, the agent nervously said, "You don't want to buy any life insurance, do you?"

"No," replied the sales manager, curtly.

"I didn't think you would," said the agent as she got up and headed for the door.

"Wait a minute!" said the sales manager. "Come back here."

"Yes, sir," said the agent, obviously nervous and frightened.

"You are without a doubt the worst salesperson I've ever seen."

The agent looked down. "Yes, I know . . . ."

"Listen, you've got to have enthusiasm when you sell—you have to be positive, not negative. You have to believe in yourself."

"Yes, sir."

"Now, look, I'm a very busy man, but I'll show you how." And for the next 30 minutes the sales manager gave the young agent all the benefits of his experience and wisdom.

"I don't know how to thank you," said the agent.

"That's all right," said the sales manager. "Now, because you're obviously new at this, I'll buy a small policy from you."

The agent quickly dug out a policy. The sales manager signed it, then said, "Remember, don't go in cold, not knowing what you're going to say. Work out a planned and organized sales presentation."

The agent smiled, "Oh, I have. What you've just seen is my organized approach to sales managers."

Before I can sell John Jones
What John Jones buys,
I must see the world
Through John Jones' eyes.

THEY USED to tell this story around the 20th Century-Fox offices in New York. The company had advertised for a salesperson and got this reply from an applicant:

"I am at present selling furniture at the address below. You may judge my sales ability if you will stop in to see me at any time, pretending that you are interested in buying furniture.

"When you come in you can identify me by my red hair. And I will have no way of identifying you. Such salesmanship as I exhibit during your visit, therefore, will be no more than my usual workday approach, and not a special effort to impress a prospective employer."

Despite hundreds of other applicants, the redheaded furniture salesperson got the job.

JOHN SMITH is still the most common name in the United States. It was for that reason that Mark Twain dedicated his story of *The Celebrated Jumping Frog* to John Smith, "whom I have known in diverse and sundry places and whose many and manifold virtues did always command my esteem."

Twain figured that anyone to whom a book is dedicated

would be sure to buy at least one copy, and since there were thousands of John Smiths, his book would be assured of at least a modest sale.

Passion persuades.

ANITA RODDICK
Founder, The Body Shop

A YOUNG PSYCHOLOGY student serving in the Army decided to test a theory. Drawing kitchen duty, he was given the job of passing out apricots at the end of the chow line.

He asked the first new soldiers that came by, "You don't want any apricots, do you?" Ninety percent said, "No."

Then he tried the positive approach: "You do want apricots, don't you?" About half answered, "Uh, yeah, I'll take some."

Then he tried a third test, based on the fundamental either/or selling technique. This time he asked, "One dish of apricots or two?" And in spite of the fact that soldiers don't like Army apricots, 40 percent took two dishes and 50 percent took one!

❖ ❖ ❖ SARCASM

A CANDIDATE for city council was doing some door-to-door campaigning, and things were going pretty well, he thought, until he came to the house of a grouchy-looking fellow. After the candidate's little speech, the fellow said, "Vote for you? Why I'd rather vote for the devil!"

"I understand," said the candidate. "But in case your friend is not running, may I count on your support?"

PLAYWRIGHT GEORGE BERNARD SHAW once wrote to Churchill:

Dear Mr. Churchill:

Enclosed are two tickets to my new play, which opens Thursday night. Please come and bring a friend, if you have one.

Churchill sent back the following reply:

Dear Mr. Shaw:

I am sorry, I have a previous engagement and cannot attend your opening. However, I will come to the second performance, if there is one.

PAUL E. MCGHEE
Health, Healing and the Amuse System
Kendall/Hunt

SATISFACTION ❖ ❖ ❖

Look at a day when you were supremely satisfied at its end. It's not a day when you lounge around doing nothing. It's when you've had everything to do and you've done it.

MARGARET THATCHER
Former British prime minister

We can achieve the utmost in economies by engineering knowledge; we can conquer new fields by research; we can build plants and machines that will stand among the wonders of the world; but unless we make it possible for our workers and our executives alike to enjoy a sense of satisfaction in their jobs, our efforts will have been in vain.

ANDREW R. STETINIUE

❖ ❖ ❖ **SECRETS**

Nothing is as burdensome as a secret.

FRENCH PROVERB

Most of us can keep a secret. It is the people we tell it to who can't.

❖ ❖ ❖ **SELF-RELIANCE**

In the game of life, heredity deals the hand, society makes the rules, but you can still play your own cards.

LAURENCE J. PETER
Canadian writer

There is no future in any job. The future lies in the person who holds the job.

What I have learned is . . . there ain't no genie. I am it. If the wealth and adventure and fame are to come, I'd better get tough on the only one who can make it happen . . . me!

TY BOYD
Professional speaker

STRANGE BUT TRUE . . .

Everybody wants a piece of the pie, but nobody wants to bake it.

Nobody owes anybody anything; it's up to each individual to set high standards for himself or herself, and to set about working hard and creating a solid future.

KATHARINE HEPBURN
Actress

To be nobody-but-myself—in a world which is doing its best, night and day, to make you everybody else—means to fight the hardest battle which any human being can fight, and never stop fighting.

e.e. cummings (1894-1962)
Poet

SERVICE ❖ ❖ ❖

Life's most persistent and urgent question is: What are you doing for others?

MARTIN LUTHER KING, JR. (1929-1968)
Civil rights leader

Service is the rent you pay for room on this earth.

SHIRLEY CHISHOLM
Former member, U.S. Congress

A PASSENGER in a dining car looked over the luncheon menu. The list included both chicken salad sandwiches and chicken sandwiches. He decided on the chicken salad sandwich, but absentmindedly wrote chicken sandwich on the order slip.

When the waiter brought the chicken sandwich, the customer angrily protested. Most waiters would immediately pick up the order slip and show the customer that the mistake was his. This waiter didn't.

Instead, expressing regret at the error, he picked up the chicken sandwich, returned to the kitchen, and a moment later placed the chicken salad sandwich in front of the customer.

While eating his sandwich, the customer picked up the order slip and saw that the mistake was his. When it came time to pay the check, the man apologized to the waiter and offered to pay for both sandwiches.

The waiter's response was, "No, sir. That's perfectly all right. I'm happy you've forgiven me for being right."

Aim for service, not success, and success will follow.

Business is a lot like tennis—those who don't serve well end up losing.

◆ ◆ ◆ **SOLITUDE**

ANNE MORROW LINDBERGH, the author and wife of famed aviator Charles Lindbergh, once made this observation:

"If one sets aside time for a business appointment, a trip to the hairdresser, a social engagement, or a shopping expedition, that time is accepted as inviolable. But if one says, 'I cannot come because that is my hour to be alone,' one is considered rude, egotistical, or strange. What a commentary on our civilization, when being alone is considered suspect; when one has to apologize for it, make excuses, hide the fact that one practices it—like a secret vice."

Shakespeare, Leonardo da Vinci, Benjamin Franklin, and Abraham Lincoln never saw a movie, heard a radio, or looked at TV. They had "loneliness" and knew what to do with it. They were not afraid of being lonely because they knew that was when the creative mood in them would work.

CARL SANDBURG (1878-1967)
Writer

SPEAKING ✦ ✦ ✦

The famous American lawyer Louis Nizer had this advice for speakers: "If you haven't struck oil in 15 minutes—stop boring."

A CLERGYMAN who hadn't seen a colleague for many years went to hear him preach. Afterward, he remarked about the change in the preacher's style. Years earlier, the preacher had been all fire and brimstone; now he was more subdued, and he seemed to say more in fewer words.

"When I started," he said, "I thought it was the thunder that impressed everyone. Now I know it's the lightning."

THE LATE Yale professor and lecturer William Lyon Phelps once said he got credit for only one-fourth of his after-dinner speeches.

"Every time I accept an invitation to speak, I really make four addresses," he explained. "First is the speech I prepare in advance. That is pretty good. Second is the speech I really make.

"Third is the speech I make on my way home, which is the best of all; and fourth is the speech the newspapers the next morning say I made, which bears no relation to any of the others."

Every speaker has a mouth;
An arrangement rather neat.
Sometimes it's filled with wisdom.
Sometimes it's filled with feet.

ROBERT ORBEN
Speechwriter

There are two kinds of people who don't say much, those who are quiet and those who talk a lot.

If your mind should go blank, don't forget to turn off the sound.

There are two ways to be clever. First, think of a bright remark in time to say it. Second, think of it in time not to say it.

ORVILLE WRIGHT, the pioneer aviator, was a man of very few words. On one occasion, Orville's friend tried in earnest to persuade him to address an important conference of scientists, but to no avail.

"I'm not a parrot," Orville said to his friend. "The parrot is the best talker and the worst flier in the bird kingdom."

A HUNGRY MOUNTAIN LION came out of the hills, attacked a bull and killed it. As it feasted on its kill, the lion paused from time to time to roar in triumph. A hunter in the area heard the commotion, found the lion and shot him dead.

The moral of the story is: When you're full of bull, keep your mouth shut.

A closed mouth gathers no feet.

Silence is never more golden than when you hold it long enough to get all the facts before you speak.

IT HAD BEEN a long, tedious meeting—so long that the chairman had to apologize to the guest speaker and inform him that he could speak for only five minutes. The room had to be vacated so that hotel employees could set up for another function.

The speaker responded to the five-minute limit with this story:

A little girl went into a store with a single nickel and asked for a candy bar. She was informed that the candy bar cost 65 cents. Then she tried to buy a soda; that cost even more. Ice cream on a stick was even more expensive.

The child left the nickel on the counter and walked sadly away. When the clerk called out to her that she had left her nickel behind, the little girl turned around and said, "Oh, that's all right. I can't do anything with it."

SPORTS ♦ ♦ ♦

THE BASKETBALL HALL OF FAME is in Springfield, Massachusetts, the city where James A. Naismith invented the game. What few people realize, though, is that though he got the credit, the invention of this ultimate team sport was itself a team effort.

In the 1880s, Springfield College was a hub for physical education, the place where coaches from YMCAs all over the country came to improve their skills. In the fall, the game everybody loved was football. But when winter's snow came, sports had to move inside, where the only activities at the time were calisthenics. Boring, the students complained.

Naismith went to the dean and pleaded for a two-week break from calisthenics to concoct a new indoor winter game. So Naismith and his students began an intense period of experimentation, with themselves as guinea pigs. Indoor football, they soon learned, was far too rough. The same was true of soccer and lacrosse, the other popular games of the day. They needed a game that would minimize roughness—hence the rule that players could not touch each other, that the ball could be touched with hands only, and that players could not run holding the ball. And no bats or sticks—that was asking for trouble inside a gym. The players would have to pass the ball to each other.

And so, day after day, Naismith and his students, through trial and error, steadily refined the game.

At the end of the two weeks, when the first fully developed basketball game was played, the only hitch was that whenever a score was made, the whole game ground to a halt while someone climbed a ladder to get the ball out of the peach basket they had fastened to the gym balcony. But that wasn't such a terrible problem that first time out: The score was just 1-0.

DANIEL GOLEMAN, PAUL KAUFMAN and MICHAEL RAY
The Creative Spirit
Dutton

———

Sports such as baseball, football, basketball, and hockey, develop muscles. That's why Americans have the strongest eyes in the world.

———

A LITTLE BOY came home from playing baseball with a disgusted look on his face. When his father asked him what was wrong, he replied, "I was traded."

"That shouldn't make you feel so bad. All the big baseball players get traded."

"I know," replied the boy. "But I was traded for a glove."

GENE BROWN
Journalist

STORIES ❖ ❖ ❖

ANECDOTES, stories, and metaphors are either Velcro or Teflon. The Velcro ones stick with you while the Teflon ones don't. Sometimes hearing (or reading) the right one at just the right time can change your life.

In *Soar with Your Strengths* (Dell), Donald Clifton and Paula Nelson tell how one Velcro metaphor had a life-changing effect on one of the world's greatest opera stars—Luciano Pavarotti. The great tenor explains:

"When I was a boy, my father, a baker, introduced me to the wonders of song. He urged me to work very hard to develop my voice. Arrigo Pol, a professional tenor in my hometown of Modena, Italy, took me as a pupil. I also enrolled in a teachers' college. On graduating, I asked my father, 'Shall I be a teacher or a singer?'

" 'Luciano,' my father replied, 'if you try to sit on two chairs, you will fall between them. For life, you must choose one chair.' "

SUCCESS ❖ ❖ ❖

If at first you DO succeed, try something harder.

ANN LANDERS
Syndicated columnist

There are four rungs on the ladder of success:

Plan Purposefully
Prepare Prayerfully
Proceed Positively
Pursue Persistently

AFRICAN-AMERICAN PROVERB

You can get everything in life you want, if you will just help enough other people get what they want.

ZIG ZIGLAR
Motivational speaker

You either have to be first, best, or different.

LORETTA LYNN
Country music singer

The road to success is marked with many attractive parking places, tempting rest stops, and forbidden U-turns. And watch out for the detours!

Success is the ability to go from one failure to another with no loss of enthusiasm.

WINSTON CHURCHILL (1874-1965)
British prime minister

We can't spell S CCESS without **U**.

Failure, rejection, and mistakes are the perfect stepping stones to success.

ALAN GOLDBERG
Sport psychologist

Your success depends on getting yourself to do what you have to do even when the "I don't want to" thoughts and "I don't feel like it" feelings get in your way.

The ladder of success may now be an elevator, but it's still self-service.

Success is 99 percent failure.

SOICHIRO HONDA
Founder, Honda Motor Corporation

There are no secrets to success: Don't waste time looking for them. Success is the result of perfection, hard work, learning from failure, loyalty to those for whom you work, and persistence . . . .

COLIN POWELL
Former chair, Joint Chiefs of Staff

Success isn't money. Success isn't power. The criteria for your success are to be found in yourself. Your dream is something to hold on to. It will always be your link with the person you are today, young and full of hope. If you hold on to it, you may grow

old, but you will never be old. And that is the ultimate success.

TOM CLANCY
Writer

The archer strikes the target, partly by pulling, partly by letting go.

Once you get rid of the idea that you must please other people before you please yourself—and you begin to follow your own instincts—only then can you be successful.

RAQUEL WELCH
Actress

ON CHRISTMAS EVE 1939, 25-year-old Geoffrey E. MacPherson was working in a cramped, rented office in the center of Nottingham, England. It was almost 10 p.m., but he had more important things to occupy his mind than the lateness of the hour.

A year earlier, he had started his own one-person business, selling yarn to the city's textile industry, yet the big orders on which he had staked his future had so far eluded him. To make matters worse, World War II had started in September, so trade threatened to become even more difficult in the months ahead.

Suddenly, the telephone rang. A major United Kingdom textile manufacturer was trying to place an urgent order for yarn—in bulk. Telephone calls to 14 well-known suppliers had already gone unanswered, the staff having long departed for their Christmas holidays.

At their 15th attempt, their call had been answered by a virtually unknown yarn supplier in Nottingham! Moreover, the young man on the other end of the line was showing himself to be only too willing to meet their critical deadline. The yarn was delivered on time, and from that day the small Nottingham agency became their main supplier.

It proved to be the major turning point in the young man's fortunes. By the end of the 1940s, he had diversified into textile machinery, and by the late 1980s, Geoffrey E. MacPherson Ltd. was among the top 100 private exporting companies in the U.K.

Mr. MacPherson remains the chairman of the company he founded over 50 years ago, and he can still be found at his desk most weekends. Few salespeople will argue with him when he asks them to travel to a distant sales area on a Sunday, or to work at an exhibition stand into the middle evening. They all know the story of the big order that arrived late on Christmas Eve!

JERRY GIESLER, a Hollywood attorney, once said, "If there is any one thing which has contributed to my success, it is the fact that I have always made myself accessible to others. I will see or talk to anyone at any time, whether at home or at the office. It doesn't matter how important the client may be who is in my office; if a call comes through for me, I get it, and no calls are ever challenged. I am never too busy to see or talk to the elevator man, the taxi driver, the porter, the lowest extra, or the biggest star in Hollywood."

THE THREE-WORD SUCCESS COURSE

EVERYTHING YOU NEED to know about success can be reduced to three simple words:

CAN WILL NOW

1. *Can.* Can you do it? Do you possess the innate ability? The truth is: Yes, you *can!* You have the same innate ability as Shakespeare, Einstein, Marie Curie, Martha Graham, and George Washington Carver. They were not born with any more raw talent than you. You have powers buried deep inside you that you haven't discovered yet.

2. ***Will.*** Will you use your remarkable ability? Just because you *can* does not necessarily mean you *will*. You have the same raw ability as a Shakespeare, but what did Shakespeare do that you haven't done yet? Through remarkable effort and perseverance, Shakespeare gained access to his remarkable ability. You can too!

3. ***Now.*** When will you begin? Many people die with their songs unsung. Right *now* take one step (even if it's a small micromovement) in the direction of your dreams.

ROB GILBERT
Editor, *Bits & Pieces*

There are no shortcuts to any place worth going.

BEVERLY SILLS
Opera star

Success is more a function of common sense than it is of genius.

AN WANG

One of the hardest things in life is to be just as enthusiastic about the success of others as you are about your own.

Success is being able to hire someone to mow the lawn while you play golf for exercise.

A successful person is one who went ahead and did the same thing the rest of us never quite got around to.

One gauge of success is not whether you have a tough problem to handle, but whether it is the same problem you had last year.

DONALD M. KENDALL, retired chairman and chief executive officer of PepsiCo, Inc., had this to say when asked what it takes to get to the top of the corporate ladder:

"There's no place where success comes before work, except in the dictionary. You can't get to the top of any profession without a lot of hard work, and I don't care whether you're in art, in music, in business, or in the academic world.

"It also requires enthusiasm and excitement about what you're doing. If you're not happy every morning when you get up, leave for work, or start to work at home—if you're not enthusiastic about doing that, you're not going to be successful."

OVER A HUNDRED YEARS ago when Gail Borden, American pioneer and inventor, was crossing the Atlantic from England, two children on board died because the milk was contaminated.

He began to dream of a way to make milk safe for shipboard use. He eventually discovered a way through a principle called "condensed milk."

When Gail Borden died, his gravestone carried this epitaph: "I tried and failed. I tried again and again and succeeded."

The secret of business success is the combination of imagination and enterprise.

JAMES C. HUMES
Speaker's Treasury of Anecdotes about the Famous
Harper & Row

We are all self-made, but only the successful will admit it.

236

The moment you commit and quit holding back, all sorts of unforeseen incidents, meetings, and material assistance will rise up to help you. The simple act of commitment is a powerful magnet for help.

NAPOLEON HILL (1883-1970)
Writer

A diamond is just a piece of coal that made good under pressure.

♦ ♦ ♦ **TACT**

"CULTIVATE TACT," Baltasar Gracián, Spanish writer and Jesuit priest, wrote three centuries ago. "It is the mark of culture, the lubricant of human relationships."

In the Middle East they tell the following story to illustrate the essence of tact:

A sultan called in one of his seers and asked how long he would live.

"Sire," said the seer, "you will live to see all of your sons dead." The sultan flew into a rage and handed the prophet over to his guards for execution. Then he called for a second seer and asked the same question.

"Sire," said the prophet, "I see you blessed with long life, so long that you will outlive all your family." The sultan was delighted and rewarded the seer with gold and silver.

Both prophets knew the truth, but one had tact, the other did not.

Tact is the ability to see others as they wish to be seen.

TALENT ❖ ❖ ❖

Most workers have a great many strengths that they can rarely get to use. Strengths can be job skills and knowledge, general abilities, or personality characteristics. Research has found that every person can do at least one thing better than any other 10,000 people. There are, in fact, a great many hidden talents in every employee.

DEAN SPITZER
Super-Motivation
AMACOM

"WHEN my daughter was about seven years old, she asked me one day what I did at work. I told her I worked at the college—that my job was to teach people how to draw.

"She stared back at me, incredulous, and said, 'You mean they forget?' "

HOWARD IKEMOTO
Art professor

Use what talents you possess: The woods would be very silent if no birds sang there except those that sang best.

HENRY VAN DYKE (1852-1933)
Writer

❖ ❖ ❖ TAXES

Sign on a New York gas station: *"We collect taxes—federal, state, and local. We also sell gasoline as a sideline."*

Bumper sticker: **Drive carefully. We need every taxpayer we can get.**

❖ ❖ ❖ TEACHERS

I have learned silence from the talkative, toleration from the intolerant, and kindness from the unkind; yet, strange, I am ungrateful to these teachers.

KAHLIL GIBRAN (1883-1931)
Lebanese novelist, poet, and artist

ONE DAY, four high school students decided to cut their morning classes. After lunch, they reported to their teacher that their car had had a flat tire. The teacher simply smiled and said, "Well, you missed the test this morning, so take your seats and get out your notebooks."

Still smiling, she waited for them to settle down. Then she said, "First question. Which tire was flat?"

ED AGRESTA
Don't Count the Days, Make the Days Count

YEARS AGO a professor gave a group of graduate students this assignment: Go to an impoverished area of town. Take 200 boys, between the ages of 12 and 16, and investigate their background

239

and environment. Then predict their chances for the future.

The students, after consulting social statistics, talking to the boys, and compiling much data, concluded that 90 percent of the boys would spend some time in jail.

Twenty-five years later another group of graduate students was given the job of testing the prediction. They went back to the same area. Some of the boys—by then men—were still there, a few had died, some had moved away, but they got in touch with 180 of the original 200. They found that only four of the group had ever been sent to jail.

Why was it that these people, who had lived in a breeding place of crime, had such a surprisingly good record? The researchers were continually told: "Well, there was a teacher . . . ."

They pressed further and found that in 75 percent of the cases, it was the same woman. The researchers went to this teacher, now living in a home for retired teachers. How had she exerted this remarkable influence over that group of children? Could she give them any reason why these people should have remembered her?

"No," she said, "no, I really couldn't." And then thinking back over the years, she said musingly, more to herself than to her questioners: "I loved those boys . . . ."

TEAMWORK ✦ ✦ ✦

Cooperation is spelled with two letters: WE.

THERE'S NO "I" IN TEAM

WHETHER YOU'RE A TEAM LEADER or a team member, it's crucial to have a "we" mind-set. Because, in sports, the best team doesn't win as often as the team that gets along the best.

Here's the critical question: Does your participation make your team a better team?

Let's look at it this way:

Imagine that your team is in a tug-of-war. To win, every single member has to give an all-out effort in unison—everyone pulling together.

Three kinds of problem people will prevent your team from winning:

#1. Participants who give an all-out effort, but don't pull in unison with their teammates. These people are doing their own thing. If they were musicians, they'd be out of rhythm, they would be out of synch with everyone else.

#2. Participants who hold onto the rope, but do not pull. These people are team members in name only. They take, but they do not give. They want all the privileges but none of the responsibility.

#3. Participants who pull in the opposite direction. These people work against their teammates and are poisoning the team with "dissension."

You can't afford to be a problem.

You have to be part of the solution.

Groups of people either **pull together** or **pull apart**. There's no in-between.

Your team can start pulling together. And it all begins with you.

Here's what you can do *right now*:

#1. Make sure you're working with your teammates rather than against them.

#2. Refuse to be **selfish**. Become more **self-less**. Give yourself to your teammates.

#3. Start looking at the situation from the bird's-eye "we" view rather than the worm's-eye "me" view.

The real benefit of a team can be found in the word "team." It's an acronym for:

Together **E**veryone **A**chieves **M**ore

ROB GILBERT
Editor, *Bits & Pieces*

THE MATH OF SYNERGY

Synergy is group   multiplied by itself! Note here that it's
the *function bet*   bers that makes the difference!

$\div 6$

$\jmath = 9$

MICHAEL SHANDLER and MICHAEL EGAN
OM! Turbo-Charged Team Building
AMACOM

Wh   *ite, they can tie up a lion.*

ETHIOPIAN PROVERB

Working together works.

I use not only all the brains I have, but all I can borrow.

WOODROW WILSON (1856-1924)
28th President of the U.S.

No one can whistle a symphony.

HALFORD E. LUCCOCK

Nobody can do everything,
but everybody can do something.
And if everybody does something,
everything will get done.

GIL SCOTT HERON
Writer

A candle loses nothing by lighting another candle.

FATHER JAMES KELLER (1900-1977)
Founder, The Christophers

It's time for us to turn to each other, not on each other.

JESSE JACKSON
Civil rights leader

The most important measure of how good a game I played was how much better I'd made my teammates play.

BILL RUSSELL
Basketball player

AN OUT-OF-TOWNER drove his car into a ditch in a desolate area. Luckily, a local farmer came to help with his big strong horse named Buddy.

He hitched Buddy up to the car and yelled, "Pull, Nellie, pull!" Buddy didn't move.

Then the farmer hollered, "Pull, Buster, pull!" Buddy didn't respond.

Once more the farmer commanded, "Pull, Coco, pull!" Nothing.

Then the farmer nonchalantly said, "Pull, Buddy, pull!" And the horse easily dragged the car out of the ditch.

The motorist was most appreciative and very curious. He asked the farmer why he called his horse by the wrong name three times.

The farmer said, "Oh, Buddy is blind, and if he thought he was the only one pulling, he wouldn't even try!"

SOMEONE ONCE ASKED the conductor of a great symphony orchestra which instrument he considered the most difficult to play.

"Second fiddle," said the conductor. "I can get plenty of first violinists, but to find one who can play second fiddle with enthusiasm—that's a problem. And if we have no second fiddle, we have no harmony!"

No one can help everybody, but everybody can help somebody.

TELEVISION ◆ ◆ ◆

I'm always amazed that people will actually choose to sit in front

244

of the television and just be savaged by stuff that belittles their intelligence.

ALICE WALKER
Writer

Television is a device that permits millions of people to listen to the same joke at the same time and yet remain lonesome.

It was bound to happen someday: On network television an announcer broke in to say, "We interrupt this special report to bring you a special report."

❖   ❖   ❖   **THINKING**

There are two kinds of people:

Those who *stop to think* and
Those who stop thinking.

What is the hardest task in the world? To think.

RALPH WALDO EMERSON (1803-1882)
Philosopher, essayist, and poet

Our life is what our thoughts make it.

MARCUS AURELIUS (121-180)
Roman emperor and philosopher

TIME ❖ ❖ ❖

Lost time is never found again.

THELONIOUS MONK (1920-1982)
Jazz musician

One thing you can learn by watching the clock: It passes the time by keeping its hands busy.

IF YOU'RE EVER going to be what you want to be, heed the words of comedian Sid Caesar:

"There are the *Nows, Was's,* and *Gonna-Be's.* A *Now* is the most precious thing you can have, because a *Now* goes by with the speed of light. Let's say you're having a beautiful *Now* that you want to hold onto forever. No matter how much you want to hold onto it, it's going to be a *Was.* A lot of people get stuck in and can't let go of the *Was's.* Those *Was's* get heavy, and they start to decay into *Shoulda-Couldas.* And they never have time for the new *Now.*

"Follow this advice and you'll be what you always felt you were *Gonna-Be.*"

---

*Take time to laugh. It is the
music of the soul.*

*Take time to think. It is the
source of power.*

*Take time to play. It is the
source of perpetual youth.*

246

*Take time to read. It is the
greatest power on earth.*

*Take time to love and be loved.
It is a God-given privilege.*

*Take time to be friendly. It is the
road to happiness.*

*Take time to give. It is too short
a day to be selfish.*

*Take time to work. It is the
price of success.*

**Half our life is spent trying to find something to do with the
time we have rushed through life trying to save.**

WILL ROGERS (1879-1935)
Humorist

❖ ❖ ❖ **TIME MANAGEMENT**

DON'T EVER SAY, "I don't have enough time."

You have exactly the same number of hours per day as Martin
Luther King, Jr., Marie Curie, Thomas Jefferson, Martha Graham,
or Bill Gates.

SELECT A LARGE BOX and place in it as many cannonballs as it will
hold, and it is, after a fashion, full; but it will hold more if smaller
matters be found.

Bring a quantity of marbles; very many of these may be packed in the spaces between the larger globes. The box is now full, but still only in a sense. It will contain more yet. There are spaces in abundance, into which you may shake considerable quantity of small shot, and now the chest is filled beyond all question; but yet there is room.

You cannot put in another shot or marble, much less another cannonball; but you will find that several pounds of sand will slide down between the larger materials; and even then between the granules of sand, if you empty yonder jug, there will be space for all the water in the jug and for the same quantity several times repeated.

Where there is no space for the great, there may be room for the little; where the little cannot enter, the less may make its way, and where the less is shut out, the least of all may find ample room.

So where time is, as we say, fully occupied, there must be stray moments, occasional intervals, and bits of time which might hold a vast amount of little usefulness in the course of months and years.

CHARLES H. SPURGEON (1834-1892)
English Baptist minister

———————————

Don't agonize. Organize.

FLORYNCE KENNEDY
Lawyer

———————————

❖ ❖ ❖ **TODAY**

We shall do much in the years to come,
    but what have we done today?
We shall give our gold in a princely sum,
    but what did we give today?
We shall lift the heart and dry the tear,
We shall plant a hope in the place of fear,
We shall speak the words of love and cheer,
    but what did we speak today?

We shall be so kind in the afterwhile,
    but what have we been today?
We shall bring each lonely life a smile,
    but what have we brought today?
We shall give to truth a grander birth,
And to steadfast faith a deeper worth,
We shall feed the hungering souls of earth,
    but whom have we fed today?

We shall reap such joys in the by and by,
    but what have we sown today?
We shall build us mansions in the sky,
    but what have we built today?
'Tis sweet in idle dreams to bask,
    but here and now do we do our task?
Yes, this is the thing our souls must ask,
"What have we done today?"

THERE ARE MANY fine things that you mean to do someday, under what you think will be more favorable circumstances. But the only time that is surely yours is the present, so this is the time to speak the word of appreciation and sympathy, to do the generous deed, to forgive the fault of a thoughtless friend, to sacrifice a little more for others.

Today is the day to express your noblest qualities of mind and heart, to do at least one worthy thing that you have long postponed. Today you can make your life significant and worthwhile. The present is yours to do with as you will.

GRENVILLE KLEISER
Writer

THERE ARE TWO days in every week about which we should not worry—two days that should be kept free from any fear and apprehension. One of these days is Yesterday, with its mistakes and cares, its aches and pains, its faults and blunders. Yesterday has passed forever beyond our control. All the money in the world cannot bring back Yesterday. We cannot undo a single act we performed; we cannot erase a single word we said; we cannot rectify a single mistake. Yesterday has passed forever beyond recall. Let it go.

The other day we should not worry about is Tomorrow, with its possible adversities, its burdens, its large promise, and poor performance. Tomorrow also is beyond our immediate control. Tomorrow's sun will rise either in splendor or behind a mass of clouds—but it will rise. And until it does, we have no stake in Tomorrow, because it is as yet unborn.

That leaves us but one day—Today! And a person can fight the battles of just one day.

Yesterday and Tomorrow are futile worries. Let us, therefore, resolve to journey no more than one day at a time.

ROBERT J. BURDETTE

❖ ❖ ❖ **TROUBLE**

TROUBLE MAKES us one with every human being in the world—and unless we touch others, we're out of touch with life.

If I had a formula for bypassing trouble, I wouldn't pass it around. Wouldn't be doing anybody a favor. Trouble creates a capacity to handle it. I don't say embrace trouble. That's as bad as treating it as an enemy. But I do say meet it as a friend, for you'll see a lot of it and had better be on speaking terms with it.

OLIVER WENDELL HOLMES (1809-1894)
Physician and writer

Troubles are like babies—they only grow if you nurse them.

The best way to meet trouble is to face it.

❖ ❖ ❖ **TRUST**

HAVING SOMEONE'S trust is like having money in the bank. Just like a bank account, you must make deposits if you expect to make withdrawals.

When you keep your word, it's like making a deposit into your trust fund. The more often you perform the way you promised, the larger your balance is. Whenever you break your word, you have made a withdrawal from your account.

You have a separate trust fund with each person that you have a relationship with. If you have been making regular deposits into your account with that individual, when the time comes that you are unable to keep your word (let's face it, nobody's perfect!), you will still have a large enough balance of trust to draw from. That person will realize that your account is still good.

You are trustworthy!

MATT DIMAIO
Motivational speaker

_____

WHEN MOST oarsmen talk about their perfect moments in a boat, they refer not so much to winning a race as to the feel of the boat, all eight oars in the water together, the synchronization almost perfect. In moments like that, the boat seems to lift right out of the water. Oarsmen call that the moment of swing.

Olympics contender John Bigelow loved that moment, but what he liked most about it was that it allowed you to trust the other men in the boat. A boat did not have swing unless everyone was putting out the exact measure, and because of that, and only because of that, there was the possibility of true trust among oarsmen.

DAVID HALBERSTAM
The Amateurs
William Morrow and Co.

TRUTH ❖ ❖ ❖

If you tell the truth you don't have to remember anything.

MARK TWAIN (1835-1910)
Writer and humorist

_____

A lie may take care of the present, but it has no future.

_____

When a thing is funny, search for a hidden truth.

> GEORGE BERNARD SHAW (1856-1950)
> Irish playwright

As scarce as truth is, the supply seems greater than the demand.

> ADLAI STEVENSON (1900-1965)
> Politician

If you want to be well-liked, never lie about yourself—and be careful when telling the truth about others.

At times it's difficult to tell
What generates the greatest woe:
The truths of us told by a friend,
Or the lies of us told by a foe.

> ART BUCK

ONCE UPON A TIME, Truth went about the streets as naked as the day he was born. As a result, no one would let him into their homes. Whenever people caught sight of him, they turned away and fled.

One day when Truth was sadly wandering about, he came upon Parable. Now, Parable was dressed in splendid clothes of beautiful colors. And Parable, seeing Truth, said, "Tell me, neighbor, what makes you look so sad?" Truth replied bitterly, "Ah, brother, things are bad. Very bad. I'm old, very old, and no one wants to acknowledge me. No one wants anything to do with me."

Hearing that, Parable said, "People don't run away from you because you're old. I too am old. Very old. But the older I get, the better people like me. I'll tell you a secret: Everyone likes things disguised and prettied up a bit. Let me lend you some splendid clothes like mine, and you'll see that the very people who pushed you aside will invite you into their homes and be glad of your company."

Truth took Parable's advice and put on the borrowed clothes. And from that time on, Truth and Parable have gone hand in hand together and everyone loves them. They make a happy pair.

BEATRICE SILVERMAN WEINREICH (editor)
Yiddish Folktales
Pantheon Books

VALUES ◆ ◆ ◆

Always do right. This will gratify some people and astonish the rest.

MARK TWAIN (1835-1910)
Writer and humorist

Sometimes the poorest man leaves his children the richest inheritances.

RUTH E. RENKEL

AN ANGEL APPEARS at a faculty meeting and tells the dean that in return for his unselfish and exemplary behavior, the Lord will reward him with his choice of infinite wealth, wisdom, or beauty. Without hesitation, the dean selects infinite wisdom.

"Done!" the angel says and disappears in a bolt of lightning. Now all heads turn toward the dean, who sits surrounded by a faint halo of light. At length, one of his colleagues whispers, "Say something!"

254

The dean looks at them. "I should have taken the money."

BETSY DEVINE and JOEL COHEN
Absolute Zero Gravity
Simon and Schuster

It is not good for all our wishes to be filled; through sickness we recognize the value of health; through evil, the value of good; through hunger, the value of food; through exertion, the value of rest.

GREEK ADAGE

SISTER CAROL ANNE O'MARIE is a nun in Oakland, California, who writes mystery novels about an elderly nun playing detective. According to Leigh Winers of the *San Jose Mercury*, Sister O'Marie was once approached by a Hollywood company to turn her novels into a television series.

She was told that it would help dramatically if the central character were younger, had a drinking problem, and perhaps had an illicit love affair before she donned the habit. When the author declined to contemplate such changes, the television producer tried the ultimate argument:

"You're turning down a chance, Sister, to make a lot of money."

"What would I do with it?" replied the nun, who had taken a vow of poverty. "I'm not going to live in a nicer convent."

PETER HAY
Canned Laughter
Oxford University Press

255

VISION ❖ ❖ ❖

VISION is a crucial component in the formula for success. It holds the keys to the future. The inspirational lives we look to for guidance remind us of this time and time again.

The following incident will illustrate our point.

At Disney studios in Burbank, California, Mike [former Disney executive Mike Vance] could gaze out of his office window, across Buena Vista Street, to St. Joseph's Hospital where Walt Disney died.

His death was preceded by an amazing incident that reportedly took place the night before in Walt's hospital room.

A journalist, knowing Walt was seriously ill, persisted in getting an interview with Walt and was frustrated on numerous occasions by the hospital staff. When he finally managed to get into the room, Walt couldn't sit up in bed or talk above a whisper.

Walt instructed the reporter to lie down on the bed, next to him, so he could whisper in the reporter's ear. For the next 30 minutes, Walt and the journalist lay side by side as Walt referred to an imaginary map of Walt Disney World on the ceiling above the bed.

Walt pointed out where he planned to place various attractions and buildings. He talked about transportation, hotels, restaurants, and many other parts of his vision for a property that wouldn't open to the public for another six years.

. . . A man who lay dying in the hospital whispered in a reporter's ear for 30 minutes, describing his vision for the future and the role he would play in it for generations to come.

This is the way to live—believing so much in your vision that even when you're dying, you whisper it into another person's ear.

MIKE VANCE and DIANE DEACON
Think Out of the Box
Career Press

All I know is that the first step is to create the vision, because when you see the vision there—the beautiful vision—that creates the want power.

ARNOLD SCHWARZENEGGER
Actor

IN ADDITION to Mount Rushmore, one of Gutzon Borglum's great works as a sculptor is the head of Abraham Lincoln in the Capitol in Washington, D.C. He cut it from a large block of stone in his studio. One day, when the face of Lincoln was just becoming recognizable out of the stone, a young girl was visiting the studio with her parents. She looked at the half-done face of Lincoln, her eyes registering wonder and astonishment and then ran to the sculptor. "Is that Abraham Lincoln?" she asked.

"Yes."

"Well," said the little girl, "how in the world did you know he was inside there?"

❖ ❖ ❖ **WALKING**

George M. Trevelyan, British historian and walking enthusiast, once remarked, "I have two doctors—my left leg and my right leg."

WALKING uplifts the spirit. Breathe out the poisons of tension, stress, and worry; breathe in the power of God. Send forth little silent prayers of goodwill toward those you meet. Walk with a sense of being a part of a vast universe. Consider the thousands of miles of earth beneath your feet; think of the limitless expanse of space above your head. Walk in awe, wonder, and humility. Walk at all times of day. In the early morning when the world is just waking up. Late at night under the stars. Along a busy city street at noontime.

WILFRED PETERSON
Writer

WILL ❖ ❖ ❖

One ship drives east, and another west
With the self-same winds that blow;
'Tis the set of the sails
And not the gales,
That decides the way we go.
Like the winds of the sea are the ways of fate,
As they voyage along through life;
'Tis the will of the soul
That decides its goal,
And not the calm or the strife.

ELLA WHEELER WILCOX (1850-1919)
Poet

People do not lack strength; they lack will.

VICTOR HUGO (1802-1885)
French writer

❖ ❖ ❖ **WINNERS**

Winners are like teabags. You never see their true strength until they're in hot water.

JOHN WOODEN, retired men's basketball coach at UCLA, is the most successful college basketball coach ever. During his 27 years at UCLA, his teams never had a losing season. In his last 12 years there, they won 10 national championships, seven of those in succession, and they still hold the record for the longest winning streak in any major college sport—88 games over four seasons.

With a record like that, we should listen to Wooden's reply after somebody asked him what he had to say about success:

"To me, success isn't outscoring someone, it's the peace of mind that comes from self-satisfaction in knowing you did your best. That's something each individual must determine. You can fool others, but you can't fool yourself.

"Many people are surprised to learn that in all my years at UCLA, I never once talked about winning. Instead I would tell my players before games, 'When it's over, I want your head up. And there's only one way your head can be up—that's for you to know, not me, that you gave your best effort. If you do that, then the score doesn't really matter, although I have a feeling that if you do give your best, the score will be to your liking.'

"I honestly believe that in not stressing winning as such, we won more than we would have if I'd stressed outscoring opponents."

A competitor will find a way to win. Competitors take bad breaks and use them to drive themselves just that much harder. Quitters take bad breaks and use them as reasons to give up.

NANCY LOPEZ
Golfer

Winning isn't everything, but it beats anything that comes in second.

PAUL "BEAR" BRYANT (1913-1983)
Football coach

WISDOM ❖ ❖ ❖

A WOMAN who had gained fame as a great dispenser of wisdom was visited one day by a delegation of men. They asked her how she had become so wise.

"When people come here," she said, "I ask them what kind of advice they want, then I give it to them. They go away convinced that I'm brilliant."

Wisdom is in the head, not in the beard.

The wisdom of life is to endure what we must and to change what we can.

MANY YEARS AGO, begins a classic Chinese story, there was a man who had a horse and one son. One day his horse broke out of the corral and fled to the freedom of the hills. "Your horse got out? What bad luck!" said his neighbors.

"Why?" the man said. "How do you know it's bad luck?"

Sure enough, the next night the horse came back to his familiar corral for his usual feeding and watering, leading 12 wild stallions with him! The farmer's son saw the 13 horses in the corral, slipped out, and locked the gate. Suddenly he had 13 horses instead of none. The neighbors heard the good news and came chattering to the farmer, "Oh, you have 13 horses! What good luck!"

The man answered, "How do you know it's good luck?"

Some days later his strong young son was trying to break one of the wild stallions only to be thrown off and break a leg. The neighbors came back that night and passed another hasty judgment: "Your son broke his leg? What bad luck!"

The wise father answered again, "How do you know it's bad luck?"

Sure enough, a few days later a warlord came through town and conscripted every able-bodied young man, taking them off to war, never to return again. But the young man was saved because of his broken leg.

A MAN said to his eight-year-old granddaughter, "I'll give you a quarter if you can tell me where God is."

The young but very wise girl replied, "I'll give you two quarters if you can tell me where God isn't."

The stupid neither forgive nor forget. The naive forgive and forget. The wise forgive but do not forget.

Wisdom can only be planted, nurtured, and harvested. It cannot be manufactured.

KIM BROUWMEESTER

AN OLD MOUNTAINEER from West Virginia was celebrated for his wisdom. "Uncle Zed," someone asked, "how did you get so wise?"

"Weren't hard," said the mountaineer. "I've got good judgment. Good judgment comes from experience. And experience—well, that comes from having bad judgment."

Wisdom consists in knowing what to do with what you know.

A proverb is a short sentence based on long experience.

MIGUEL DE CERVANTES (1547-1616)
Spanish writer

The person who wrote "a job well done never needs doing again" has never weeded a garden.

One furnace melts all hearts—love;
One balm soothes all pain—patience;
One medicine cures all ills—time;
One light illuminates all darkness—hope.

IVAN PANIN

A handful of common sense is worth a bushel of learning.

WORDS ❖ ❖ ❖

DOCTRINES, credos, manifestos, laws, declarations, codes of ethics. Ever since people have been able to communicate, they have compiled words to live by. But the world is still troubled.

Take these words: honesty, workmanship, ambition, faith,

education, charity, responsibility, courage. Chances are four and a half billion people won't agree to live their lives by them.

But think how much better your life would be if just one person does. You.

From an advertisement for
United Technologies Corporation

Cold words freeze people, and hot words scorch them, and bitter words make them bitter, and wrathful words make them wrathful. Kind words also produce their own image on men's souls; and a beautiful image it is. They soothe, and quiet, and comfort the hearer.

BLAISE PASCAL (1623-1662)
French mathematician, physicist, and philosopher

Handle them carefully, for words have more power than atom bombs.

PEARL STRACHAN

❖ ❖ ❖ WORK

How do I work?
I grope.

ALBERT EINSTEIN (1879-1955)
Physicist

The effect of sustained hard work is unbeatable. You can overcome all faults through hard work. I've seen that happen both

personally and to people all around me.

PHILIP GLASS
Composer

Nothing is really work unless you would rather be doing something else.

J.M. BARRIE (1860-1937)
Scottish writer

I BELIEVE the one rule that is definite and applies to everyone is that you need sweat and pain and a lot of hard work, and then it has to appear effortless.

I remember reading something Ginger Rogers said once in *The New York Times* when they were doing a salute to Fred Astaire. She said that at many rehearsals their feet would bleed.

Remember how easy it looked? That's high artistry!

TONY BENNETT
Singer

Too many people are ready to carry the stool when there is a piano to be moved.

Doing nothing is the hardest work of all.

**Work will not guarantee you anything.
Without it you don't stand a chance.**

PAT RILEY
Basketball coach

I WENT TO SEE "Magic on Broadway" with the amazing illusionist Joseph Gabriel. When the show ended, a young boy sitting in front of me said to his father, "Dad, this is the greatest show on earth!"

I went to see the show on a Saturday when there were four performances. After the second show, I interviewed Joseph. I asked him where he found the enthusiasm to do four high-energy shows in one day (plus two more on Sunday and four more during the week).

Joseph said he had three reasons for being so "into it." First of all, he said he loves performing magic. Second, he feels very grateful to be able to make his living doing something he loves. And third, he said you never know who's in the audience.

These three reasons give Joseph Gabriel a passionate commitment to his profession.

You're probably not a magician, but no matter where you are "performing," you have a "stage." It might not be on Broadway, but you can perform your special type of magic in an office, a classroom, or a store.

So if you want to put on "the greatest show on earth," it all starts with passion, gratefulness, and expectancy.

ROB GILBERT
Editor, *Bits & Pieces*

---

*Every morning I get up and look through the **Forbes** list of the richest people in America. If I'm not there, I go to work.*

ROBERT ORBEN
Speechwriter

Make the work interesting and the discipline will take care of itself.

E.B. WHITE (1899-1985)
Writer and humorist

Never get so busy making a living that you forget to make a life.

Thank God every morning when you get up that you have something to do that day which must be done, whether you like it or not. Being forced to work, and forced to do your best, will breed in you temperance and self-control, diligence and strength of will, cheerfulness and contentment, and a hundred virtues which the idle never know.

CHARLES KINGSLEY (1819-1875)
English clergyman and writer

Those footprints on the sands of time were made by work shoes.

The one important thing I have learned over the years is the difference between taking one's work seriously and taking one's self seriously. The first is imperative and the second is disastrous.

DAME MARGOT FONTEYN (1919-1991)
British dancer

Thunder is good, thunder is impressive, but it is the lightning that does the work.

MARK TWAIN (1835-1910)
Writer and humorist

Work to become, not to acquire.

The legendary comedian Milton Berle defined a committee as a group of people who "keep minutes and waste hours."

◆ ◆ ◆ **WORRY**

"WHAT WE NEED here," said the boss to the job candidate, "is a head worrier—somebody to do the worrying instead of me. The job pays $60,000 a year. Do you think you can handle it?"

"Certainly," said the candidate. "When do I get my first check?"

"That," said the boss, "is your first worry."

The reason why worry kills more people than work is that more people worry than work.

ROBERT FROST (1874-1963)
Poet

Cheer up! Remember today is the tomorrow you worried about yesterday.

"Don't tell me that worry doesn't do any good," said the overworked executive. "I know better. The things I worry about never happen."

INDEX

273